WILLARD SCOTT'S
THE JOY OF LIVING

WILLARD SCOTT'S

THE JOY OF LIVING

Coward, McCann & Geoghegan / New York

Library of Congress Cataloging in Publication Data
Scott, Willard.
Willard Scott's the joy of living.

1. Scott, Willard. 2. Meteorologists—United States—
Biography. I. Title
QC858.S37A35   551.5'092'4   [B]   82-4956
ISBN 0-698-11130-3   AACR2

PRINTED IN THE UNITED STATES OF AMERICA

This book is dedicated to
the people of my old First Baptist Church
in Alexandria, Virginia,
who taught me the real meaning
of love and the importance of passing it on to others.

I want to offer a special word
of thanks to Pam Proctor, who helped me
organize my thoughts and get this book on paper.

Contents

Foreword

If you're looking for sex, violence, intrigue, crime, passion; if you happen to think that margarine tastes as good as butter; if you can't tell the difference between freshly brewed coffee and instant and really don't care; if you have to be the best-dressed person and have the latest fashion; if you're truly a highly sophisticated person who never does the wrong thing but who always makes the right move at the right time; if you never have to apologize because you never have anything to apologize for—then this book is definitely *not* for you.

However, if you believe in black-eyed peas on New Year's Day; if you love the smell of a wood fire; if you cry when you watch old movies; if you feel sad when you see a wounded bird; if you love your mother and father and would never think of hurting anybody; if you love homemade biscuits, a sip of Jack Daniels, mashed potatoes and meat loaf, you just might find something in the following pages that hits home.

With that out of the way, let this foreword begin a look backward at this good ol' Southern Baptist boy who joined a union, moved north, and found happiness on the *Today Show* in New York City.

CHAPTER 1

True Confessions

I want to set the record straight from the very beginning about the kind of guy I am. I cuss, I drink a bit, I lust in my heart, and I've fooled around a little bit so I know what it's all about.

On the other hand, I haven't done that many evil things in my life. I believe in telling the truth.

I try not to be a hypocrite, so don't bother looking in the closet for skeletons. I'll tell you up front what I am.

One thing about me—I have an incredible ego. While I'm a hail-fellow-well-met and always have been in the halls and on the air and in everything else that I do, I always, constantly, have been concerned with me—number one.

In some ways it's a terrible handicap that comes back to haunt you. You can become so wrapped up in yourself that it can drive you crazy, make you mean, and alter all your relationships. This broadcasting business I'm in has a tendency to do that to people, and I've tried to fight it all my life.

When it comes to the sophisticated world of TV, I'm a mutation. If you put me on an audition tape, everything is wrong, except for the fact that I have a nice voice. On radio I have no trouble. But if you were to look at my résumé, you'd see that I'm forty-eight years old, I'm bald, I'm overweight, I don't make all the smooth moves, and I dress like a slob.

I'd never come out of a computer as being a hit. Yet, here I am on the *Today Show*. I take tremendous pride in the fact that I beat the system. I don't belong in any textbook. There's no format or category I fit into. I'm me.

My mother said in a baby book I had that when I was three months old I used to smile in my sleep. I don't know what I was doing or thinking. All I know is that I've always been happy.

There's never been any reason why I shouldn't be happy. I've always been able to make the best of whatever the cards dealt me. But I admit I've been dealt some pretty darn good cards. I've had great health, I've had total, absolute, complete love from every member of the family, I've had excellent breaks, and I've taken advantage of all those things.

Why didn't I become a drunk? Why didn't I leave home? I can't answer that. Maybe it has something to do with all those country people I sprang from. But I'll let the story tell itself, and you can make your own judgment.

14

CHAPTER 2

Why I Believe in Ancestor Worship

The Japanese do it. The Chinese do it. So do the American Indians. And in my own way, I believe in it too. I'm talking about ancestor worship.

Of course, different people go about it in different ways. The Japanese, for example, get down on their knees once a year and open a little bronze altar in a place of honor in their house. There they pay homage to all those folks whose genes they bear, whose personalities they reflect, and whose funny little quirks they carry on.

In Ghana, on the other hand, people celebrate the anniversary of a relative's death with a big feast and invite the whole town. They slaughter a cow, beat lots of drums, and pour libations of whiskey on the ground.

All this wining and dining is done to curry favor with the souls of departed relatives going back two and three generations. The whole ceremony is kind of an insurance policy to prevent the deceased from getting annoyed and to make sure they take good care of those still on earth.

Now, I'm not one for pouring good whiskey on the floor or falling to my knees and bowing to the ghost of Grandma Emma, bless her soul. But I am for paying respect to all those folks who made me, Willard Scott, the kind of guy I am today. There's something sacred about a family relationship with all its roots deep in the past. It's the bulwark of the whole civilization. And you can't deny that you are what you are because you have been molded by all those people down the line.

When you come right down to it, there isn't any single unit that's more important than the family. It's been that way since the time of Abraham and it will be that way forever. There are some things that just don't change, and the family is one of them.

Take it from me, if you want to begin to get joy out of life, don't bother to go on a safari, climb the Great Wall of China, or take a tanker to Pago Pago. There's joy right in your own backyard, starting with your family tree and those ancestors of yours who have been resting six feet under for decades and centuries.

I come from a long line of dirt farmers over in North Carolina. They were all mountain people, from up in the Blue Ridge Mountains. We can trace my mother's father's family, the Phillipses, back to the early 1700s when they first came to North Carolina. They were all simple farm people, English and Scotch-Irish mostly. Woodruff was my maternal grandmother's maiden name. My father, of course, was a Scott, and his mother was a Greer. So we had Woodruffs and Phillipses, Greers and Scotts. All farmers. Just folks. But there was a life in them, a sparkle, a certain twinkle. I guess it was in the genes.

I don't recall one member of our family who was a sourpuss. My father had six sisters and one brother and my mother had two sisters and five brothers. As far as I know, even farther back down the line, there wasn't a grump in the whole family. We were all basically an unsophisticated, simple lot.

There are people like Uncle Paul, my mother's brother, who was late for his own high school graduation. I had locked him in the outhouse and he couldn't get out. Finally, he had to break down the door. But by that time he had missed the school bus and ended up getting to school in the middle of the ceremonies.

On the face of it, my family may not sound much like a group worth "worshipping." After all, there was nobody famous in the bunch and very few of them had any formal education worth mentioning.

But I'm not talking about putting my folks or yours on a pedestal. The important thing is to get down to a practical knowledge of your people, knowing who you are and where you belong. That's what my kind of ancestor worship is all about.

With that knowledge of your forebears, you can begin to reap the joy that was sown by generations before you. That positive feeling comes first of all from the stability of being rooted in the past. Second, it comes from being honest about yourself and accepting your personality, and physical characteristics, warts and all. Third, it comes from belonging to a family that

17

accepts you without question. And finally, it comes from faith—like that old hymn puts it, "Faith of our fathers, living still."

To begin with, one of the greatest joys that I've gotten out of musing about my ancestors is the stability that all that family history brings. The stories about the Scotts and the Phillipses that I've heard from my childhood are more than just homey reminiscences to me. They're a living part of me, and they have given me perspective on my own limited time here on earth.

Early on in life I had a sense that there was more to me than just me. Maybe it had something to do with my visits to Uncle Richard's house in North Carolina. I grew up in Alexandria, Virginia, but every now and then we'd go back to North Carolina to visit my mother's family homestead.

Uncle Richard was my great-uncle, my grandfather Phillips' brother. He had a nice big old farm with a classic Southern farmhouse way up on a hill. It wasn't an antebellum mansion with big white columns on the porch, or anything like that. But it did have a big verandah to catch the breeze and some wrought iron around it. And it had a nice view overlooking the river, which was actually nothing more than a creek.

The old house had bullet holes in it from a Yankee visit during the Civil War. As the war was winding down, Sherman's troops came up through South Carolina and North Carolina and did more of the same thing they had done in Georgia: They burned almost everything that crossed their path. What's more, my grandfather Phillips used to tell me that what the Yankees didn't eat, they took with them. Our house escaped the flames, but it didn't escape the looting. When they came by my great-great-grandfather's house, they stole all our hams and all of our food. And for some reason, this Yankee soldier went and put a couple of bullet holes in the kitchen. But those Yankees never put the torch to the Phillips' homestead.

Uncle Richard was real proud of those holes, and some of that Southern pride rubbed off on me. As he would talk about those Yankees, my eyes would get all wide and my chest would swell with pride that our house still stood and that my great-great-grandaddy had fended him off. Sitting in that kitchen, I felt as though I were transported back there, staring down at that Yankee as my grandfather had. And just knowing that I sprang from those strong Southern roots made me stronger somehow.

Along with those bullet holes, the family cemetery plot up on the hill behind Uncle Richard's house gave me a sense of stability. I had a sense that others had gone on before me and would go on after me, and that I was part of something lasting.

One of the sad things about modern times, it seems to me, is that family plots are gone. In the old villages, you couldn't walk more than four or five blocks and not be in a churchyard with a cemetery. You were constantly aware that people were in the ground.

If you had any brains at all, you'd realize that those people at some point got dressed, walked around, had sex, went to the bathroom, brushed their teeth, had colds, enjoyed a fire, and had a drink. And it would remind you that this life is a stopover period. To me, a cemetery is a constant reminder that life is all too short. And just thinking about that helps me keep perspective.

In our family plot were three or four generations of Phillipses going back to the 1700s. The freshest grave was the one where my great-grandmother had been laid to rest. I never knew her, but I felt I had some kind of relationship to her and to the others buried next to her, through my grandparents.

I spent a lot of time around that cemetery plot when I was visiting Uncle Richard. He had a wild cherry tree just above the plot, and my cousin and I would spend hours up in that old tree, eating cherries and peering down over the generations of Phillipses buried beneath us. The roots of that wild cherry tree were entwined with those graves, and so were the roots of my identity.

As I sat in that tree, spitting cherry pits down on great-great-grandfather Phillips, I had a strong feeling for who I was. And that brings me to the second reason I believe in ancestor worship: Knowing who these folks were brought me face to face with who I was and helped me to size up myself honestly.

I know I'm a character. But I also know *why* I'm a character. That's because I've gotten my personality, weaknesses and all, from all those Phillipses and Scotts before me. And that has helped me understand myself and my two daughters better.

In my mind, there's no question about it: You *do* pass personality traits on from generation to generation. But instead of being burdened by the bad traits, if you recognize them you can work to improve yourself and your life. If you can accept yourself honestly, then you can learn to play to your strengths.

From the Scotts I inherited a streak of honesty—the kind of honesty that's characterized by straight talking and straightforward living. They'd tell you exactly what they thought. They were basically good, uncomplicated country people who didn't bother about non-essentials.

Let me give you a picture of what the Scotts were like. Grandmother Scott was a big, heavy woman whom I take after in my frame and mind set. She and Grandpa T. P. Scott had a little old house outside North Wilkesboro, North Carolina.

My grandfather worked in a feed store—a real country feed store. I can remember going down to see him at the store when I was about six or seven. What I remember most is the little birds that would fly all around the store. They had a field day because they had a freeload off the feed—bins and bins of oats, barley, chicken feed, and horse feed that had a wonderful sweet smell. The horse feed had the best smell of all because it was made with molasses and corn.

Grandfather Scott used to make whiskey. I never saw him make it, but my father swore that somewhere there was a five-gallon barrel buried on that old place.

Whenever we visited my grandfather, we'd follow the same routine. First we saw him down at the feed store. Then my father would take me to the Coca-Cola bottling plant where my uncle, T. P. Scott, worked. Every town in the South worth anything had a Coca-Cola bottling plant, and it was a big deal to go visit.

In the factory, they would pass a little high-powered light and magnifying glass past the Coke bottles to make sure there were no funny little spiders or anything else caught in there. It was like candling eggs, an age-old process that involves holding a candle behind an egg to check for impurities. After this, Uncle T. P. would give me cold Coca-Cola and I would watch him work in the factory.

The Scotts were so down to earth that they did without things even though they could afford better. On some nights we might have a "syrup sandwich" for dinner. It was like poor people. They weren't that bad off, but they enjoyed taking a slice of bread—soft, spun bread full of air holes—and smearing it all over with homemade butter. Then they'd load it down with syrup—good old Log Cabin syrup. It tasted like uncooked French toast.

That's the way the Scotts did things: plain, simple, and honest.

Perhaps the most honest Scott of all, though, was Aunt Zanie. She lived back up in the woods of North Carolina and until World War II she didn't have any electricity. She lived in one of those old mountain homes. She had a loft where she went to sleep because the heat rose up there. And she had old pine floors and a fireplace. That was her only heat. She had a wood-burning "cook stove" to cook with, and a flatiron to iron with.

That life all changed right after World War II when the Rural Electrification Act put power lines back in the country. Around '47 or '48 they got power back to her cabin, and to celebrate, her kids bought her a new GE electric iron. A few days after they gave it to her, they came back and asked how she liked it.

"I threw the thing out the window," she said.

When her kids asked why, she said without apology, "The darn thing wouldn't get cold." She had forgotten to pull out the plug.

There was a certain charm to Aunt Zanie's directness. My father, Herman, on the other hand, could be straightforward to the point of being crude about it.

I don't go that far, but I'm a pretty honest fellow. I'll

22

put up with a lot of nonsense where it's not important, but I won't where it's important. I've been known to get tough and stick to my guns, no matter what the consequences. That's a Scott trait through and through. I'm also a Scott when it comes to my tastes, although mine aren't quite as simple as a "syrup sandwich." But at my home in Virginia, I'd rather spend my time shooting the breeze with the guys at the hardware store than getting duded up for a star-studded event with the local gentry.

From my mother's side of the family, the Phillipses, I was blessed with a big dose of what my wife, Mary, calls, "the capacity to be happy." We all have it to one degree or another, but some folks just tend to see more sunshine than rain in life. That was how it was with the Phillipses.

They were a lively bunch. I look a lot like my grandfather Phillips, except that he wasn't fat and he wasn't quite as tall as I am. There wasn't an ounce of fat on him. He had stubble for whiskers—he shaved every third day or something. He was a farmer, first over in North Carolina and later up in Maryland, where he bought a small farm around 1918.

All of my mother's brothers were so darn much fun. Even today when I think about them I feel good. I can see them sitting around my grandmother's kitchen table at the farm in Maryland. We'd always have about ten or twelve of us there. They were a little loud, but they were fun. There was a brightness to them. Their eyes flashed, and they were all a bit bug-eyed.

I remember Uncle Tommy. I dearly loved him. He also had those incredibly pronounced eyeballs. He was one of the more intelligent members of the family. We used to speak reverently of him because he went down to Raleigh and attended the opening of the state legislature.

A lot of the warm feeling we had around my grandmother's table is what I try to project on television to this day. That whole group created a certain atmosphere that made you feel good. They were fun to be with. They were down to earth, and they laughed a lot. There was a positive thing there.

I know I've got some of that. But I also know I've got some of the Phillips' weaknesses. Like my mother, I have good common sense, but I don't have any logic at all when it comes to putting things together or following instructions.

In my case, the trait showed up most in my academic performance. I barely scraped through school. In fact, one of the few A's I ever got in my life was in science, and my schoolwork for that grade was done in typical Phillips fashion. The teacher had told us to go to a place where there was life swarming around—a stagnant pond, or whatever—and bring in a sample. Well, I took a mason jar out into the barnyard where the cow manure was. I got a jug of the stuff and brought it back to science class. They examined it under a microscope, and of course it had a lot of action in it. I guess it's appropriate that the only A I ever got was from a pile of manure—which some people have said has followed me through life.

What all of those Scott and Phillips traits add up to is me. Over the years I've come to appreciate and enjoy all those little parts of my personality that come from someone else.

But along with helping me accept myself, ancestor worship has also given me another great joy in life: an incredible sense of belonging.

In my family, if you were in the family, you were really "in." No matter what you did or how far out you were, you were accepted. A good example was my great-uncle Dave Woodruff. He was my grandmother Phillips' brother. A lot of the Woodruffs were from Tennessee and western North Carolina. But for some reason or other, he ended up going down to Texas and being a doctor. He had gotten divorced, and his wife had taken him to the cleaners.

Later on, though, he headed east. Somewhere along the line there must have been some weaknesses in the vascular system of some of the Woodruffs, because he gradually became senile. I saw this weakness in a painful way with my own mother who died senile.

But at my grandfather's farm in Maryland, Uncle Dave was accepted, weakness and all. It all started the day my grandfather got a call from the police up in Baltimore. They had found Uncle Dave in a park half naked. He was wearing an undershirt and a hat and was walking around like he didn't know where he was. My grandfather and uncles went up to get him. They piled into my grandfather's '40 Pontiac which he kept in a shed. He had driven it once and it went off the road, so he never drove it again. The only reason he kept it was that he felt he should have a car. This was one time he was glad he had it.

They brought Uncle Dave back to the farm and he stayed there for about a season and a half. In the summer he would just sit there at my grandmother's big dinner table and groan. He was a big son of a gun who would eat cucumbers and beans by the ton.

One day Uncle Paul looked at him and said, "You know, Uncle Dave, all you do is eat and belch."

But every now and then, Uncle Dave showed he

knew the score. He came down with a rash around his ankle once and the folks took him to every doctor around. He washed the rash in calamine lotion, bathed it in baking soda, and did everything else the doctors told him. But he couldn't get rid of it.

Then one day, in one of his more lucid moments, he barked, "Bring me outside."

He went out, dug up some kind of root, and put it on his rash. It went away in two days.

To the family, Uncle Dave wasn't an embarrassment. He was just Uncle Dave, a lovable old coot if there ever was one. What I learned from seeing Uncle Dave's acceptance by my family was that I, too, would always belong. There would always be a place where I would fit in and where I would be loved, no questions asked. The knowledge that I belonged somewhere gave me incredible confidence and strength.

To me, that's really what the joy of living is all about. It isn't an emotional high that crashes with the first bad break or disappointment. It's an undergirding of positive support that can carry you through the good times and the bad. And all of that comes, first of all, through your ancestors: from the stability of deep roots, an honest understanding of your own character traits, and the security of belonging to a family.

But I wouldn't be completely honest if I didn't admit that there's one more way ancestor worship has given me the kind of joy I've been talking about. And that's through faith.

I mean, when you go back far enough—before the Phillipses and the Scotts—you end up with the one ancestor who started it all: God.

And like King David, who had his share of personality flaws, I can't help but be overwhelmed that I'm part of God's family.

Let's face it, if you want stability, imagine being part of a family tree that goes back to Adam and Eve. If you want to accept yourself honestly, consider the characters like Moses and Paul God had to put up with over the years and loved in spite of themselves. And if you want to feel like you belong, just look at the crowd of tax collectors, hookers, and cowards Jesus called his brothers and sisters.

When I realize I'm part of God's extended family, I can't help but feel worshipful toward my number one ancestor. I'm part of God's creation, and I'm proud of it.

Maybe that's why I've gotten so much joy out of the rest of God's creation, which I learned about firsthand on my Grandfather Phillips' farm in Maryland.

CHAPTER 3

The Land of Johnny Appleseed

One of my all-time great heroes in life is Johnny Apple-seed. You remember Johnny. He was the guy who went around the country planting apple trees. His real name was John Chapman, and he was born in Massachusetts in 1774. Somehow, Johnny got it in his head that the country needed apples, and he made it his personal mission to go out ahead of the western migration and plant trees.

Starting in western Pennsylvania, he moved through Ohio and along the way planted apple trees, thousands of them, over hundreds of acres of virgin country.

Eventually he ended up in Fort Wayne, Indiana, where he died in 1845. But behind him he left a legend-ary trail of good deeds, like the time he traveled thirty-six miles through the woods at night to bring help to Mansfield, Ohio, which was threatened with an attack by Indians.

But such a feat would have been considered all in a day's work for Johnny. What made him larger than life was his passion for God's creation—the wildlife and the land and all that grew on it—and his sense of gratitude for it.

It didn't take much to make him happy. He didn't need a Cuisinart to make applesauce in a minute, or a night out in the Big Apple for entertainment, or designer jeans with an apple on the rear to do his work in.

All he needed was the basics: the sun, the rain, and the appleseed. With these simple tools, and his extraordinary zeal, his life bore fruit.

Now, the reason I relate to Johnny's story is that it pretty much sums up the lessons I learned as a kid on my grandfather's farm. My grandparents had a small dairy farm above Baltimore in a little town called Freeland, Maryland. It's right up on the Pennsylvania-Maryland border, on the edge of Pennsylvania Dutch country. Until I was about twelve, my family went up to the farm almost every weekend, and everything I love about the country today I've gotten from that experience.

Up on the farm, my grandparents lived the life of simple country people. The only money they made was from their milk. My grandfather made forty to eighty dollars a month at most—this was back in the thirties and forties. It was a big deal when they got indoor plumbing after World War II. Prior to that time you knew you had to transact some big business if in the middle of the night you got up to walk that eighth of a mile down the road to the privy.

For small jobs, the chamber pot was kept under the bed. Every time I mention "chamber pot," by the way, I'm reminded of the story we used to tell about the two old guys who were reminiscing about the good old days growing up in the country.

One guy says to the other, "I sure do miss the old chamber pot."

"That's no surprise," said the other. "You always missed it when you were a kid."

This kind of life was basically a throwback to the way Johnny Appleseed and the first settlers lived in this country and the way people lived in Europe for hundreds of years before that. It hasn't been more than about seventy-five years since this whole way of life has gone down the chute.

But it hasn't completely disappeared. I consider myself a kind of missing link to this era, which is little more than a quaint bit of history to most folks today. What links me to the farm is more than nostalgia for the past and an abiding love for chickens and the smell of fresh cow poop. The strongest pull I feel is the tug of the honest values of simple living that the farm—and Johnny Appleseed—represented.

Now, it may not be fashionable to talk about simple living nowadays, at a time when everyone's trying to get more out of life—more money, more free time, and more status. And I must admit that I enjoy the good life as well as anybody. I like the limousine that takes me to work and the swimming pool in my backyard, and the ego boost I get when I'm recognized by all sorts of people around the country.

But I've discovered in practice what all those theologians and philosophers have been saying for years in theory. And that is that none of those things is worth a hill of beans when it comes to lasting joy. What counts in life is appleseeds. That's right—appleseeds.

Even when you discount all the legends and tall tales surrounding Johnny, one thing still comes through loud and clear: Johnny's life meant something. He had something that's rare in today's world—a sense of being needed, which infused his life with purpose. That sense of purpose gave him joy in his work, repetitious and boring as it must have been planting all those seeds day in and day out. It also gave him a sense of gratitude to his Creator for all that he had.

Those same values that gave meaning to Johnny's life were planted deep within me as a child. And like his appleseeds, which blossomed into beautiful fruit trees, those values are the seeds of joy in my life today.

You see, in a peculiar way the farm *was* Johnny. It was a living embodiment of his personality: cooperative, industrious, and humble. Everywhere you looked, he seemed to be peering around the corner, beckoning you to partake of the joys that were there for the asking.

One of the things Johnny was known for was his cooperative spirit. To paraphrase another famous John, he didn't ask what others could do for him, he asked what he could do for others—whether it was giving away his shoes and walking barefoot, or pitching in to help the residents of one Ohio town build a public road. He simply saw that people needed him. And he responded with everything he had.

It was the same way on my grandparents' farm. Take my grandmother, for example. There wasn't a mean, selfish bone in her body. She was up at 4:30 A.M. with my grandfather and uncles, fixing breakfast while they milked the cows. The wood stove had been banked the night before, and all she had to do was stir it up and stick a couple of sticks of wood in and the stove was hot enough for her to bake in.

When the men came in at 7:00, she'd serve them up a breakfast of fresh eggs, country ham my grandfather had cured, and rolls and biscuits she had just baked.

If my grandmother ever wondered about her purpose in life, she never said so out loud. But the truth of the matter is, she didn't have to. She knew she was part of something much bigger, a cycle of cooperation that moved from the farmhouse to the fields, embracing every man, beast, and growing thing along the way. She saw she was needed, and like Johnny, she responded with everything she had.

It seems to me that these days we've gotten so selfish. We're more independent than we've ever been. We all have our little apartments, and our little air-conditioning units, and our little cars and our little subways. We're all in our own little worlds, and we seemingly don't need each other.

On the farm, though, everybody and everything was part of a unit that needed each other. All my grandparents had was the simple, everyday things of life: their family, their work, and the fruits of God's good earth. But there was that feeling of interdependence and cooperation to sustain life. Everything you needed for life was right there and you shared in it and gave to it.

For me, that spirit of cooperation is symbolized by the old springhouse that stood out behind the house. That was the place where the springs ran out of the ground, providing the farm with life-giving water. You encase the springs in concrete, make a trough, and put a roof over it. The icy-cold water comes out of the springs, runs through the trough and out through an overflow.

Everything has some significance: The overflow is loaded with watercress to eat; the trough is where they would put the milk to keep it cold at night. Anytime you wanted you could go up and get a cold glass of buttermilk—you'd put in a cup and just dip it out. Or you could have one of the watermelons or cantaloupes my grandfather stored there, along with the butter and cheese.

To me as a child and even to this day, it was the most perfect spot in the whole world.

From the springhouse, the cold water flowed to the kitchen of the big old farmhouse, which was the hub of life on the farm. The house was probably half kitchen, which is what everybody wants to have today. Another thing people are going back to is a wood stove. It seems kind of ironic to me that I've lived through a period when something was a necessity, then almost became semiextinct, then became quaint, and finally became an energy-saving necessity again.

An electric light bulb hung over the kitchen sink, and under the sink was slop for the hogs. Slop may sound like something dirty, but actually it's nothing more than a bucket that you fill with table scraps, grain, and sour milk to feed the hogs in the evening. It was a quick way to recycle leftovers and make sure that nothing was wasted, a practice Johnny Appleseed certainly would have approved of. In fact, one story goes that Johnny got his dander up when he saw some pieces of bread in a slop bucket outside the door of one Ohio matron. He roundly chastised her, saying that the "Gifts of a merciful God should never be thriftlessly misused."

Now, I don't know if anything edible ever slipped into my grandparents' slop bucket inadvertently, but I do know that everything on the farm had a practical use. The farm was a working farm in every sense of the word. If you needed bread, you didn't go to the store to buy it. You went to the barn and dipped into a big bin to get a scoop of homemade flour. If you wanted tomatoes, you went to the basement of the house, which had big thick stone walls and huge bins filled with potatoes and tomatoes that my grandmother had canned.

The only thing I remember they bought was clothes, Clabber Girl Baking Powder, cocoa, sugar, coffee, BC headache tablets, and Arrow Beer, which was the local Baltimore beer. And of course, they bought Lifebuoy soap. We used to take a bath in front of the old wood stove in a #3 washtub and that wonderful soap smelled so medicinal. Everybody knew you were clean because you *smelled* clean.

The house had a basement and two floors. My cousins and I slept on the second floor, with as many as four of us to a bed. Now that was real cooperation! Under the bed was a chamber pot. The mattresses were made of horsehair, and the pillows were made from chicken and duck feathers, all left over from the farm. It's like I said: *Everything* on the farm had a purpose.

That sense of cooperation was even more apparent on the day the combine came through to thrash the wheat. The man who owned the combine would go from farm to farm, following the wheat from the Shenandoah Valley on up through Maryland. You had to get the work all done in one day, because the next day he'd take the operation to the next farm. As a result, everyone pitched in to help.

It was an old-fashioned American scene. My grandfather and uncles would go out and cut the wheat, harvest it, and bring it in. Then when the old steam combine came in, they'd put in the wheat, and the machine would throw the straw in one direction and the wheat in another. It literally separated the wheat from the chaff. Then it ground up the wheat and made flour. Grandpa Phillips paid the man money or in kind with some of the flour.

Just like in the old movies, my grandmother would fix a big dinner for everybody who had worked. And at the end of the day, tired as everybody was, you had a good feeling knowing that you had been needed. Without every hand helping, a season's worth of wheat might have gone down the drain.

But it wasn't only the spirit of cooperation that gave the farm a sense of Johnny's presence. It was also through the industrious daily labors of my relatives that Johnny sowed his seeds of joy.

Johnny's style of work was anything but leisurely. He didn't just take a sack of seeds and scatter them aimlessly as he wandered through the beautiful countryside. His technique, according to his biographer Peter Smith, was to set up camp, clear some land, and plant a nursery on some of the hundreds of acres of real estate he had bought for himself. In order to pay for the land, he had to make sure it earned a profit, and that meant planting a whole lot of trees and finding folks to buy them. When the planting was done, he'd make his rounds, visiting neighbors, doing good deeds, and selling apple tree seedlings.

Rain or shine, Johnny always had plenty of work to do. And so did all country people like my grandparents.

I once asked an old farmer, "I guess you look forward to rainy days because you'll have nothing to do?"

"Hell," answered the farmer. "If you don't have anything to do when it's raining, you're not farming."

Somehow, on the farm work never seemed like work. The reason was the attitude the folks took toward it. Doing chores and milking cows and hauling hay wasn't drudgery. It was something worth getting out of bed for, even before the sun was up. That attitude has stuck with me to this day, whether I'm doing jobs around the house or appearing on the *Today Show*.

Let me take you back for a moment and show you what a typical day was like. My day on the farm started at 4:30 A.M., which is still the time I get up today. It was my job to go out with the old police dog and round up the dairy cows, about forty of them.

The dog was wonderful, and he knew his job. All I did was go out with him and watch him bark at the cows. The cows knew what they were supposed to do too. The dog and I just let them know it was time to do what they were supposed to do. With the dog barking at their heels, they all came to the barn, where my grandfather and the boys put them in the stalls and milked them.

The whole business of milking took about an hour and a half, and I loved every minute of it. The first thing they did was wash the cows good with a solution. They'd wash the udders, and then they'd take a milk stool and sit down. I mimicked everything they did.

You'd sit on this stool and stick your head in the cow's stomach to keep your balance. Another reason you did it was that the cow's tail was swishing flies. If you stood out away from the cow, the tail would constantly hit you. So the closer you got into the cow, the better. I got real close.

For every four cows my uncles milked I'd milk one, because I wasn't very good at it. But gradually I learned

36

how to do it. There's a certain rhythmic action you get when you milk a cow—it's a combination of a squeeze and a pull.

When you really got good at it, you could get fancy. One of the great sports used to be to take a cow's teat, get a good stream of milk going, and squirt the face of one of the two thousand cats that always seemed to be hanging around the barnyard driving you crazy with noise. My uncles were great at it. And the cats loved it. They'd lick each other's heads because they had milk dripping from them.

What made the whole milking process even more wonderful was the smells. There was good old cow poop—which I think is the cleanest smell in the whole world—all blended in with the aroma of cow feed in the stalls and the fresh milk in the cans.

When you finished milking, you'd dump the milk in five-gallon milk cans. Usually we ended up with four or five of them, amounting to about twenty gallons or so of milk. Then we'd carry the cans to the springhouse to mix the morning milk with the evening milk, which had been kept cold from the night before.

The best part was yet to come, though. We put the cans in the back of an old '29 Ford that had no backseat and no brakes, and then we hauled them up to the milk stand next to the mailbox at the side of the road. A truck from the dairy would come by to pick up the milk for processing.

Every ride in that rattletrap was an adventure. The only way you could stop the car was to throw it into second gear and let the clutch out fast, and it would come to a dead stop. I learned to drive on that car on some of those milk hauls when I was only about ten.

By the time the milking was done, it was 7:00 and we all headed for the house for breakfast. The kitchen had a huge table that sat twenty-five or thirty, and some of us would sit on benches and some on chairs. My grandfather always had a chair.

Afterwards, he'd take the slop bucket and go down to feed the hogs. That was a sight. I used to love to sit and listen to hogs eat. I still do. And like everything else, those hogs had a purpose: They were being raised for next year's ham.

The only real leisure of the day came when grandfather would sit around and listen to the news on the old Philco he had bought for twelve dollars. He listened to WBAL in Baltimore.

But he couldn't sit still for long because there were all sorts of chores to do. I did everything he and my uncles did. If it was midsummer, they'd make hay. They'd hitch the horses to the wagon and go out in the fields. Grandfather didn't have one motorized tractor—everything was horsepower. For a mower, he used a sickle bar hooked to a horse, and after the hay was mowed, a rake would come along pulled by another horse. My uncles would rake the hay and pitch it with a pitchfork onto the wagon. It was hard work, hot and hard, but it was fun.

Next we'd go and plow the fields. They grew wonderful vegetables and wheat along with corn and soybeans for the animals. After all, you didn't eat soybeans in those days, and we didn't know about byproducts or plastics. When the plowing was through, it was time for dinner, and then we'd spend the afternoon back out in the fields, doing whatever it was that we did. In the winter, the biggest thing was to take care of the cattle and gather wood with big handsaws. Toward evening, we'd milk the cows again and put the milk in the springhouse until morning.

Day in and day out the pattern was pretty much the same. But instead of being bored by the routine, I was caught up in its rhythms and exhilarated by the fact that like Johnny Appleseed I had so much *important* work to do.

Johnny's sense of hard work and cooperation may have given the farm its practical pleasures, but it was his humility that imbued it with a joyful spirit.

His idea of comfort was to throw up a lean-to, eat a potato hot from the fire, and walk around barefoot with a tin pan on his head and a raggedy pair of pants on his legs, even in the dead of winter.

Biographer Peter Smith tells of the time two young men came upon him in the middle of the woods miles from civilization. He was sitting in front of his make-shift shelter, cooking a potato and and looking happy as a clam.

Said Johnny, "I could not enjoy myself better anywhere. I can lay on my back, look up at the stars and it seems almost as though I can see the angels praising God, for he has made all things good."

Now, that sounds a lot like the way my grandparents looked at things. They had a certain basic appreciation for what they had. Their sense of gratitude to God for the little things in life wasn't talked about a whole lot. But it was there just the same.

It seemed to me that every day on the farm was Thanksgiving. During the war, my father had enough gas stamps to get us up to Maryland on weekends, but it was tight. Once we got there, though, it was like there was no war on. There was plenty of food—no such thing as rationing.

At dinner, the table overflowed. There was always corn, tomatoes, ham scraps left over from breakfast, maybe some fried chicken—although that was usually a Sunday dish—and lots of bread, rolls and homemade jams and jellies. There was never a whole lot of meat, but you never noticed that. What I remember is the vegetables: squash and string beans, pickled beets, lima beans, and peas. I loved them all, even as a kid. Of course, the whole dinner was topped with homemade apple and pumpkin and berry pies.

But there was much more than food to be thankful for. Going to the farm on weekends was like having my own personal Disney World to escape to. I don't remember ever going to a movie. I didn't have to. Everything I could have wanted was right there and it cost practically nothing.

Sometimes my cousin George and I would stay up all night and camp in the fields. Or maybe we'd go fishing and make our own fishing lines out of string with a safety pin for a hook. We'd add a piece of bacon fat to the hook and catch fish in the creek. If we got tired of that, we could always dam up the creek and swim in it.

For big thrills we'd go back in the woods where thick, heavy vines grew on the huge trees. We'd take an ax, cut the vines at the bottom, and then go up on top of a hill and swing down thirty or forty feet, just like Tarzan.

At other times, I'd get to go "fish gigging" with one of my uncles down at Gunpowder Creek, which runs into Chesapeake Bay. We'd go out all night with a flashlight and wade through pools in the creek, spearing the big fish as they swam by.

If we wanted to have a really big time, my cousins

and I would walk to the country store two miles away. Every weekend we'd make at least one trip to the store. We'd hike over the fields and through the woods, and if we were lucky we'd see a deer along the way, or maybe some wild turkeys. All we had was a few pennies in our pockets, but we'd come out of that store with a sack of candy. They were two for a penny: big round jawbreakers, peppermints, and Mary Janes (that was before it meant marijuana). And there were little Cokes. In those days they didn't have humongous Cokes like we do now. You bought a Coke for a nickel and got six ounces, which was just enough to wet our whistles for the trip home.

It was all of these little things, on just seventy-five acres of land, that added up to a joyful existence seven days a week. But there was one day especially when that sense of thanksgiving enveloped the whole house. That was Sunday, when the whole family got together and just plain reveled in each other.

There were three girls in my mother's family: my mother, Thelma, and her sisters Mary Nell and Mabel. And then there were five boys: Paul, David, George Reeves, Clarence, and Richard. They all lived within five or six minutes of each other, and on Sunday they brought their wives and kids over to the farm.

After the cows were milked and the chores done, we all got dressed up and went to church. We piled into three or four cars, and a caravan of Phillipses headed down the road to the Gunpowder Falls Baptist Church. The church was one of those one-room affairs, where they had curtains that drew shut over the pews to make Sunday school classes. Then they'd open them up and we'd all stay for the church service.

At home, after a big family dinner, everybody moved

into the parlor, a real honest-to-goodness parlor which was used only for Sundays.

The parlor was a special place because that's where my grandfather kept the old RCA wind-up victrola and player piano my mother had given him. Before I was born, she got a job working in Washington and made a few bucks. Some of the money went into the victrola and player piano. That was all the entertainment we ever needed. On Sundays, the big thing was to sit and listen to the piano play "Listen to the Mockingbird."

Those were the humble pleasures of life that Johnny Appleseed would have appreciated, even though that player piano might have been a bit too highfalutin for him.

But for me, all of the ordinary things we had to be grateful for every day on the farm were summed up in a real Thanksgiving Day we spent there in 1939. That was the day Aunt Mabel married Bill Keenan in the parlor of the old farmhouse.

The preacher stood in the parlor right next to the player piano, and before he had finished the ceremony it started to snow. It snowed and snowed all during the wedding service and the dinner afterwards. By the time the bride and groom were ready to leave to catch a train to Philadelphia, about thirteen or fourteen inches had fallen.

Although the train was five miles away, it was clear that nobody, not even the bride and groom, was going to drive away from the farm. Every car was stuck.

With all those shiny symbols of modern progress bogged down in the snow, it took a humble, old-fashioned solution to carry the day. Grandpa went out to the barn and hauled out a sled he hadn't used in twenty years. It was all beat up—just a one-horse deal—but it was a sled. He hitched it to an old dapple gray, bundled Aunt Mabel and Uncle Bill under a blanket, and sent them on their way.

As the honeymoon couple took off for the train across the snow-covered fields, the family stood in the door waving goodbye.

Now if all this sounds a little unreal, like some kind of quaint Norman Rockwell painting sprung to life, you're partly right. You see, as wonderful as the farm was to visit every weekend, it wasn't always so wonderful getting there. Sometimes it took a little bit longer than expected for my family to leave home in Alexandria, Virginia.

On Friday nights, my mother and I would be standing at the door waiting for my father, Herman, who more often than not was "acting ugly."

CHAPTER 4

Herman the Hillbilly

My father and mother were both from western North Carolina over in Wilkes County. They were raised about ten miles apart and knew each other as children back in 1910–15.

But my mother's father would never let her hang around with Herman because when he was ten or twelve he cussed and chewed tobacco. My grandfather didn't think he was worth anything and didn't want his daughter fooling around with him.

One day, when he was eighteen years old, Herman was plowing with a mule and said, "The hell with it." He walked away from that mule and hopped a train to Danville, Virginia, where he got a job with the Dan

River Mills Company. That's the way he told the story anyway.

I don't know how long he worked in the factory down there, but someplace along the line he ended up in Washington, and he put himself through Strayer Business School there. The first thing I remember him doing was working for Sands and Company, the Southern Railroad's Company store. He was something like a store manager. That's what he was doing when he married Thelma.

Her family had left North Carolina around 1914 and gone to Abingdon, Virginia. From there, my grandfather moved up to Maryland, where he bought his farm. My mother went to a school right outside Towson. Then, like Herman, Thelma left the farm and went to Washington. She lived in a rooming house on 14th Street and worked for the telephone company as an operator.

Thelma hadn't seen Herman for about ten years until a mutual friend from North Carolina got them together again. Herman still cussed and chewed tobacco, but this time my grandfather wasn't close at hand to put a stop to their romance.

I've got a letter dating from 1927 which Herman wrote to his boss asking for money to get married and set up housekeeping. I think he wanted a thousand dollars. That was a lot of money in those days. I'm not sure why he needed so much since they had a pretty simple wedding, but he got it.

Herman and Thelma were married by the Reverend Dodd in the Baptist Church on King Street in Alexandria, Virginia, which is where I was born and raised.

I was born on March 7, 1934, one minute to midnight.

It could have been either March 7 or March 8. When my mother asked the doctor what the actual time was, he said it was one minute before. So it stayed March 7. The only other time I was in the hospital was when I had my tonsils out.

Actually, to hear my father's cousin, Guy Scott, tell it, it was a miracle I was born at all. Apparently, my father was very upset when he heard my mother was pregnant, and he even tried to have me "taken care of." Whether there's any truth to that I'll never know. But I do know that Herman was a practical man, and he surely wondered how in the world he was going to raise a kid during the Depression.

But no matter what his attitude about me before I was born, after I arrived on the scene Herman was as devoted a father as there ever was—in his own way, that is.

He was a country boy, who was as honest a human being as God ever put on the face of this earth. And he was always honest with me. But he could be crude to the point where he could embarrass you, and he drank too much, which made him feisty and mean sometimes. But unlike a lot of fathers who acted that way, he would always make it up. You never doubted for a minute that he was with you.

If I was sick, he'd bring me little presents to cheer me up, a little dime-store nothing like a comic book or a tracing book. When I got older and had a part-time job as a page at WRC in Washington on weekends, he'd drag himself out of bed, even though sometimes he was so hung over he could barely move, and drive me across the river. Then he'd come back and get me at six. Another thing about Herman, he never missed the school plays or graduations. He might be half-loaded and a little loud or boisterous, but he showed up. No matter what came up, he always let me know I could count on him. He never let me down.

Of course, he did all of those traditional things that fathers do, like play Santa Claus. One Christmas in particular, Herman was half-fried and was doing the Santa Claus bit, trying to put tab A into slot B to get something ready for me under the tree. And he was cussing up a storm.

I woke up and Mother came up to close the door. She didn't want me to hear all that.

I remember asking her why Santa Claus was in such a bad mood.

Even if he was a little crusty at times, there was just something about Herman that made him fun to be with. I wasn't the only one who felt that way.

Alexandria in those days was like a small town, and everybody knew Herman as a happy, gregarious guy. He had a naturalness about him that could just make people feel at home, even at funerals.

Usually you walk into a funeral parlor and find everyone standing around looking morose and mumbling. Herman would walk in, go up to the widow, and say, "Helen nobody was more damn fun than George." He'd praise the guy to the sky, and talk about how much fun they had playing poker and boozing it up. If anybody was embarrassed by his boisterous approach, he'd at least give them something to talk about so they weren't standing around staring at their feet and not doing a darn thing. At the very least, Herman started things rolling.

He kept things rolling in our neighborhood, too. At first, we lived on Chapman Street in a duplex apartment, which was just the top floor of an old house.

When I was about three, we moved to Commonwealth Avenue in a little row house where I was raised. The house cost $4,750. It's worth about $120,000 now, and the neighborhood is still nice after all these years.

Our house was open twenty-four hours a day, with people coming and going. It was a zoo. Many's the time the police would come by the house after they got off duty and have a "clucker" as Herman would call the drinks they downed together.

Herman's connections with the men in blue often came in handy, like the time he was out one night and drank too much. As he was driving along the Mount Vernon parkway, he fell out of his car and it ran over his arm. The police found him and took him to the hospital to have him fixed up. They hung around the hospital until he was ready to go, then they brought him home to make sure he was safe. Alexandria was just the kind of place where people would do a little something extra. And Herman was the kind of guy to inspire such devotion.

His easy way with people made him an ace insurance agent. Around 1938 he left Sands and Company and got a job with Metropolitan Life which he kept for thirty years until he retired. He had a good head for business and made good money in those days. And he worked hard at it. Every morning he'd be out of the house by a quarter to nine. Then he would come home for lunch. Around 4:30 he'd be home for dinner, and then he'd go back out again. That was the time he could do most of his selling.

In those days you bought insurance with a fifty-cent-a-week payment. Nobody had the money to pay for a year in advance. You'd buy a thousand dollars of whole life—it was called "burial insurance"—and when you died, you had enough to pay for your burial and that was it. That's what everybody did.

Herman would carry these big green debit books, and he'd go around to people he sold insurance to and collect their fifty cents every week. A lot of the time, he'd take me with him. It was a social outing. You'd stop by and get a cup of coffee, and have some bread or cookies someone had just baked. He'd sit there and sling the bull for twenty minutes and then they'd give him fifty cents and he'd write a slip and hand it to them.

These people weren't wealthy people by a long shot—most of his customers probably made about three thousand dollars a year. And in some cases, they missed their premiums. Maybe a guy was out of work, or someone gambled and spent all the money. When that happened, Herman would pay their premiums, even for as much as six months or a year. Of course, even though he had a good heart, he had ulterior motives, too. He didn't get paid if the policy had been canceled or allowed to lapse.

More than once somebody came by the house after their spouse had up and died to find that their burial insurance was still in force because Herman had paid the premiums. They thought he was the greatest thing since sliced bread.

As for me, I thought Herman was the best father a kid could have. He was my number one hero in life, and I wanted to be like him and be with him every chance I got. Whatever he said, I took to heart.

We were driving down the street one time and he was cussing out people right and left, yelling "You son of a bitch" and "You bastard!"

I finally turned to him in confusion: "Everyone looks

the same, Dad. I can't tell the difference between a son of a bitch and a bastard."

When I was about five, he taught me how to swim. He took me out in a boat on Pretty Boy Lake, a reservoir with the Baltimore Water Supply near my grandfather's farm. We got in a rowboat, and when we got to the middle of the lake he picked me up and dumped me overboard.

He hadn't been drinking at the time. That's just the way he did business. He used to call me Charlie— "Hard Rock Charlie." All I remember of that swimming lesson was him yelling, "Swim, Charlie, swim."

Believe me, I swam.

Herman's advice about sex was just as direct. I was about twelve and was going on a date. Herman was half tight, but he got in the car to drive me to see my girl-friend.

His lesson was simple. He pointed to his crotch and said, "This thing has gotten me in more trouble than anything else I can think of. Whatever you do, don't get this girl in trouble." And that was the beginning and end of my only sex education.

With Herman, life was always an exciting adventure, and I looked forward to the times he'd let me tag along with him on his rounds, especially if he was heading for the Alexandria dairy. The dairy was owned by a guy named Mike Berchal who was my father's best customer and best friend. He bought a million-dollar insurance policy from Herman. That policy was the crowning glory of Herman's insurance business.

Herman liked to hang out at the dairy, and some Saturdays he'd let me come along and run through the place. The raw milk was brought in from the country to

the dairy, where it was heated up, processed, pasteur-
ized and bottled.

They also made ice cream. The ice cream mix would
trickle down over these huge cooling plates. It would
get cool as it came down and then it would go into some
sort of beater. But before it went to the beater, I would
go over to the cooling plates with a cream pitcher and
take all I wanted. It was like a milk shake, literally a
cascade of milkshakes. I was in "hog heaven."

On other Saturdays, though, the scene wasn't quite so
heavenly. Herman would go down to the dairy alone
and hang around with the guys. One of them was a
drinking Berchal, and he and Herman would get
together back in the dairy and knock off some of the
sauce.

Meanwhile, my mother and I would be back home
waiting for Herman to take us to my grandfather's
place in the country. At ten o'clock in the morning
we'd be ready to go, and he might not show up until
two or three. When he did show up, he was pretty well
bagged.

It was times like these that Herman started "acting
ugly."

By nature he had a strong streak of malcontent in
him. He had a tendency to find fault with people and
with situations and to never be quite satisfied with
what he had.

I have a little bit of that. My mother used to say that
when she took me to an amusement park and I'd be
riding the roller coaster, I'd start crying because I'd see
the merry-go-round and want to ride it instead. That's a
typical childish thing, but a lot of people carry it
through life. Herman was one of them. I don't know

where Herman got it from, because neither my grand-mother nor my grandfather was like that. He must have gotten it somewhere further back.

When Herman got into one of his moods, though, he became cantankerous and ornery, and anyone who came into his path was fair game for his abuse.

Once we were in a nice Italian restaurant, having dinner, when Herman started getting bugged by the music of the strolling violinists. All of a sudden he started screaming at the musicians to cut down the noise so he could eat his meal in peace. We all went through the floor.

Every now and then his feistiness got him in big trouble. One night my parents were going out to din-ner with Herman's cousin, Guy Scott, his wife, Mildred, and Ira, who was Guy's cousin from another side of the family. They started out at our house with a bottle of Early Times, hooting and hollering it up, and then they went down to King's Chinese restaurant. A couple of hours passed, and then I heard all this commotion going on in the living room after they got back from dinner.

It turns out that my father and Ira had had a fight. Herman had made some disparaging remarks about Ira's wife's character, and Ira punched him in the mouth. I never saw what happened then. But somehow Herman, Guy, and Ira all ended up getting locked up, and Mildred and my mother had to go down and get them out of jail.

At least once a month I became Herman's target and got a whipping for some prank I'd pulled. He never beat me for the sake of beating me. I'd pour sand down his gas tank or paint somebody's wall. It was normal kid stuff. But he overreacted. Still, I never felt any bitterness toward him for that.

The only thing he ever did that I resented was bullying my mother. He was a domineering guy that way, and it showed up most when he was drinking. Then he'd belittle her, or cuss her out. When he got mad at her, he always used to call her "George"—that was her father's name. He loved her more than anything in this world, but he had this dark streak in him that he just couldn't control.

Strange as it may seem, they were as close as two peas in a pod, and you can't understand Herman without understanding Thelma. In contrast to my father, Mother was all gentleness and light. I could build a religion around her. She never said a word against Herman, even when he was acting ugly. If she had just picked up a chair or a pot and hit him over the head one time, things might have been different. But she wasn't the kind to make waves.

One time, when I was about seven or eight, I saw him hit her when he had had too much to drink and she cried. At the time, I hated him for that, and I begged her to leave him. But she wouldn't even consider it. She was willing to put up with his abuse because there was too much else about Herman to love. I guess when you come right down to it, she got what she wanted and he got what he wanted.

Thelma was almost too good to be true, a melodrama-type heroine who could seem like Miss Goody Two-Shoes. She was always cheerful and upbeat, but she wasn't phony about it. That's just the way she was. She gave compliments to everyone around her because she genuinely loved people. And she gave that positive and encouraging kind of love to me every day of my life.

After I was born, she quit her job at the telephone company to devote herself to me. That's the way I looked at it anyway. As far as I could tell, she made me feel like I was the reason she was put here on earth. When I came home from school, Thelma would be in the house waiting for me. More likely than not, she'd be chatting away with one of the neighbors. She liked to play bridge and she had all these girl friends. One was Lady May Morretz. Thelma and Lady May had been childhood friends in North Carolina, so they always had a lot to talk about.

Our neighborhood was the kind of place where you could walk into at least a dozen houses and open the icebox and help yourself. My friends were always welcome in my home. I never had to worry that my mother wouldn't like it because they'd mess up the kitchen floor. She always made them feel like it was their house, too.

My mother's big social thing was the Baptist Church. She always went to the Circle meetings, and to the Bible-study classes. But religion was a private thing with her. I don't remember her throwing herself on the floor and kneeling by her bed every night or telling me to "Ask God about it in prayer."

What I do remember is her example. There was always that positive guidance there. You just knew she was getting strength from somewhere to keep up her spirits day after day.

In little ways she communicated that positive outlook on life to me. Every night before I took my bath she would read me a story. Looking back on it now, it seems like every one of those stories had an upbeat message.

One of my favorites was the *Little Engine That Could.* That's the one about the engine that tried to pull a broken-down train full of toys over a mountain even though it had never done anything like that before. Other engines, bigger and stronger ones, had refused to tackle the job. But the little engine took on the job with enthusiasm. As it moved up the mountainside, the little train huffed and puffed, and it said over and over to itself, "I think I can, I think I can, I think I can."

And by golly, it did it! Through sheer willpower and determination, the train made it over the mountaintop and delivered the toys to the kids waiting on the other side.

I heard that story over and over again, and each time I got a big charge when the train made it. Little by little the message sank in that I, too, could do anything I wanted if I believed in myself and was willing to try.

That same sort of encouragement filled Thelma's voice when she read from a big book of Bible stories. It's one of the few books from my childhood I still have. There were stories like Joseph and his coat of many colors, and Isaac and the well.

The one about Isaac made a big impression on me. The way the story goes, Isaac went out and dug for a well, and everywhere he dug, someone would come along and say, "You can't dig it here, it's my property." It happened like that four or five times, and Isaac's servants started getting pretty tired of being pushed around.

Now, the way Isaac handled the problem was not through any kind of violence, like beating someone over the head, or trying to take his land. Instead, he just kept on going mile after mile until he finally found a spot where he could dig the well without bothering anybody. After he dug that well, the folks who had given him such a hard time about the other wells came to him to make peace. They realized that anybody with that kind of persistence must have something going for him.

How did old Isaac respond? He threw them a big sit-down dinner and let bygones be bygones.

Maybe the reason I loved the story so much was that it reminded me of the things I loved about my mother. Isaac's approach to life was a lot like Thelma's: She was gentle and patient, and at the end came out a winner.

There was a softness about Thelma that kind of rounded out Herman's rough edges. Together they gave an incongruous stability to my life. I mean, here's a kid who from the time he was born had absolute unequivocal love from the two people he cared about most in this world. The knowledge that your parents are with you one hundred percent has got to be one of the biggest confidence-builders in the world. For me it was and still is.

I had what every kid wants and needs: parents who let me know that I was a VIP in their lives. I had Herman, who took me places and talked to me and put himself out for me. And I had Thelma, who literally bathed me in love.

Thelma and I had this regular little ritual every night after my bath. By that time it was long after dinner, the stories had been read, and the warm bath water was making me kind of drowsy.

I'd step out of the tub, and Thelma would wrap me up in a big old towel to dry off. Then she would walk over to the toilet seat, put down the lid, and sit on top, holding me close to her on her lap.

I would snuggle up close, my mind filled with the

happiest thoughts as I felt the warmth of her arms around me. Gently she'd rock back and forth, and I'd feel myself drifting off to sleep.

The last sound that I remember hearing was her sweet voice, singing me to sleep with Brahms' lullaby.

Now that's what I call love. That's security. That's real, honest-to-goodness joy.

CHAPTER 5

That Old-Time Religion

Any kid who's ever spent any time around a Southern Baptist church gets his chance on stage at least once a year at the Christmas pageant. I always liked that sort of thing. My big stage experience came the year I played a wise man.

You know the scene: Mary was at the cradle, Joseph stood there next to her, and in front were the three wise men. One had a crook in his hand, one had the incense, and one was kneeling. I was the kneeler.

I had on my father's bathrobe and a fake beard, and just as the curtain opened, I realized there was a pencil stuck behind my ear. I made a quick decision to cup my hand over it so people wouldn't see it.

After the show was over, somebody came over to me,

patted me on the head, and said, "You're such a clever little boy. Such stage presence. It looked like you were listening for the baby Jesus."

I may not have been listening for Jesus on that particular occasion, but I learned from an early age to listen and look for miracles in my life. Somehow, at critical times something or someone has always seemed to pop up to steer me in the right direction or get me out of a tight squeeze.

One of my tightest squeezes at the First Baptist Church came when I was twelve years old and had just started taking communion. In the Baptist church, they serve grape juice rather than wine, in tiny little individual-sized plastic cups.

On this particular occasion, I was trying to get the last bit of juice out of the bottom of the cup with my tongue, when all of a sudden the suction grabbed hold and my tongue got stuck in the cup!

I tried desperately to pull that doggone cup off, but after the first couple of tries, it wouldn't budge. Then, before I could make another attempt, the pastor asked everyone in the church to hold hands with the person next to him and sing "Blessed Be the Tie That Binds." But *I* was the one in a bind. Here I was with this cup on my tongue, and the people next to me had grabbed my hands.

But just when it seemed like I was about to be discovered, I had what I can only regard as a divine inspiration: I sucked the whole cup into my mouth and held it there until the hymn was over. Then, while no one was looking, I reached in and pulled it off my tongue.

Now, this may not sound like much of a miracle to you. But as a kid of twelve, I knew I had been saved from devastating embarrassment. That's the way it's been throughout my life. Call it what you will: Maybe I was born under some lucky star, or maybe I was blessed with an incredible sense of timing, or maybe these things just happened.

But I know it didn't "just happen" that I was at the First Baptist Church on King Street when Dr. Ernest F. Campbell held sway. I wish everybody in the world could have gone to that church and heard him preach.

He was about six feet four inches, a fine figure of a man, and he used to preach in a Prince Albert coat. When that man got up in that pulpit, and when he got fired up and tears rolled down his cheeks, you *believed*. Whatever that man said, you believed.

Sure, he'd preach a little brimstone and fire. And he'd weep sometimes. But basically he would preach the Bible stories. In the Baptist Church you'd hear the same stories over and over again. They were straight from the Scriptures and not from any psychological or sociological theme relating to something "important." They didn't relate to anything. They just *were*—pure Scripture.

Underneath it all, though, Dr. Campbell taught the one thing that there is to teach—love. The whole message was love. It all got back to the same thing. When he stepped down from the pulpit it was more of the same, love and a whole lot of hugs. To be swept up in the arms of that huge bear of a man was the closest thing I knew to heaven.

He had tremendous compassion. Somebody got sick or somebody died, and he'd come by. He was not like a lot of ministers these days who don't know how to handle such situations. In fact, a lot of them don't even show up. But Campbell was always the first there.

He didn't just pat your hand and as an afterthought throw in some words like "Ah, he's home with Jesus in the land of glory—he's in a better world."

Instead, he'd sit there and hold your hand and weep with you. He knew how to console people. Sometimes he'd say nothing.

It was his human contact, his warmth, that people responded to. He gave, and you just gave it back.

Even Herman adored Dr. Campbell, which was another reason I knew Campbell was all right. In fact, Herman liked him so much that he decided to join the church. He converted from the Methodist Church, and when I was thirteen we were baptized together. We were the only father and son to ever be baptized there in the same baptismal pit at the same time for more than one hundred years—since about 1840 I think.

In a Baptist church they have a pool right out in front of the church. Other people were being baptized at the same time. Everybody was in robes, and at the third verse of "Just As I Am Without One Plea," I walked forward.

Herman was already up there, because he was joining by what's known as a "transfer of church letter," which meant he had already made a commitment. But I was a first-timer. I had planned on it. It was a decision I made at that time in my life to accept Jesus.

I think Campbell dunked Herman first, then he dunked me. I don't remember any great dramatics. I didn't hear any cannons roar or fireworks go off or angels sing. Somehow, it just seemed like doing it together was the right thing to do. It fit right in with our relationship.

Herman's baptism may have seemed a little out of character, with all his hard drinking and cussing, but that's just the way he was. To hear him talk, you'd think he was on the same level with the best Baptist preacher. He went to Sunday School every Sunday when we were in Alexandria. But I can't say he was a traditional Baptist.

Between Sunday School and Church everybody used to go outside and chat a little bit. You had a half hour between acts. Like a lot of others, Herman would reach in and pull out a pack of Camels as soon as he hit the sidewalk.

But there was this one zealot, a slow-talking Southern boy in his teens, who just couldn't cotton to Herman's smoking. He walked up to Herman and handed him a little leaflet on the hazards of tobacco that said, "Dear brother, I see you enjoy smoking." Herman took one look at it and told the guy to get the heck out of there and leave him alone.

The irony is that a few years later Herman had to stop smoking when he got emphysema and could hardly breathe anymore. What's more, the Surgeon General of the United States spent thousands of dollars to come up with a report that ultimately said something like "Dear brother, I see you enjoy smoking." So the simple message that young Baptist was trying to get across turned out to be right after all.

Despite an occasional eager beaver, though, Campbell's church was mostly filled with folks like him, who would more likely give you a hug than a tract. There were people like Mrs. Earle Draper, a tall, thin woman who wore little flowered dresses from Montgomery Ward. I bet she paid all of $3.95 for them. She lived in a little house in Alexandria, one of those $2,000 jobs that Herman collected 50 cents from for the "burial insurance."

Mrs. Draper adored and loved me and I was incredibly receptive to the affection she radiated. She always sat in the third pew every Sunday, and after church I'd go up to say hello and she'd give me a great big hug. That meant more to me than going to church.

But the person who had the biggest influence on me at that church was a man named Reno, who was my Sunday School teacher when I was in junior high. He was a stocky guy, around five feet eight inches, with a swarthy complexion. He had kind of a Gene Kelly look about him.

What impressed me was that there was a softness about him, a gentleness. He wasn't funny. He wasn't glib. He wasn't colorful like my grandfather, or flamboyant like my father. But there was something about him that spoke to me.

It was just the way he talked about things. There were about six of us guys in his Sunday School class. We'd be sitting there in our little shirts with the tight collars sticking straight out. And he'd be talking about girls and making out and going to bed and sex, things that were considered pretty risqué at the time.

But he never presented it as dirty. He never said it was evil, or that your hands were going to drop off if you did certain things. He talked about all of it in relation to respect and the sanctity of marriage. There was not even a mention that you might get somebody pregnant and the embarrassment of it all. Instead, it was all couched in terms of an almost chivalrous respect for women. It was all positive. There wasn't one "don't" or one negative. That's what I remember, anyway.

He was my Sunday School teacher for only about two or three years. But it was the timing that was so important. He got me at that critically important age when my values were being set. Take yourself or anybody at twelve or thirteen. All of a sudden you get in with a certain crowd and their values get you started on a track you can't change. If you start messing around at twelve or fourteen, you'll be likely to mess around for the rest of your life.

My crowd was the crowd who bought Reno's line. We didn't have to be dragged to Sunday School. We loved the stuff.

And what we heard in Sunday School from Reno was reinforced by the De Molay. It's kind of a junior order of the Masonic. In fact, it was formed by the Masons, and we used to have meetings at the Masonic Lodge up on the hill, which was the highest spot in Alexandria.

The De Molay had some beautiful teachings. One of the things it preached was respect for life, and especially respect for women. There was a big emphasis on respecting your mother and other men's sisters. And they taught the old line of honesty. We also did projects, like cleaning up the baseball diamond or raising money for orphans and old people. And there would be two or three parties and hayrides.

It also had a secret side to it which I never got much of a kick out of, but I went along with it anyway. The business meetings had all these rituals with secret handshakes and secret greetings. Even now I can't talk about it in detail because it's against the rules. Members who were officers had certain trappings and went through various rituals at the beginning of a meeting. There were about twelve positions, or stations, and you sat in chairs. The guy who was in charge sat up on a throne-type thing.

The De Molay had a female counterpart called Job's Daughters. We'd have dances together which were

My friend and partner Eddie Walker, at WRC Radio.
Photograph by Ernie Newhouse.

Below left, Willard the Clown, 1959. *Below right,* "Commander Retro," a doomed kiddy show of 1963. Lester, the dog, could tell. *Photographs courtesy of WRC-TV.*

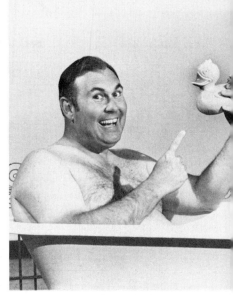

Above left, a Joy Boy in 1968. Mary had the sweater made for me; there were a lot of cold sheep that year. *Photograph courtesy of WRC-AM Radio.* *Above right*, "Ask Willard, he'll do anything!" A publicity shot in D.C. *Photograph courtesy of WRC-TV.*

News Center 4 in Washington, D.C. Left to right: Dan Daniels, sports; Glen Rinker, anchorman; Carol Channing, who helped with the weather that day; myself, and Jim Vance, co-anchor. *Photograph courtesy of James Weaver.*

Mary and Willard, 1974. *Photograph courtesy of James Weaver.*

Herman. *Photograph courtesy of James Weaver.*

The first Ronald McDonald and family: Mary, Sally, and Mary Jr.
Photograph courtesy of James Weaver.

supervised by members of our group. For every De Molay who had a yen, there was a Job's daughter who was ready. I'm sure plenty of them jumped in the backseats of Chevrolets and made out like blazes—while I'm sitting in there listening to all that stuff they were preaching at De Molay and church and wondering if I was an old dummy taking it to heart.

I remember the serious thoughts that were going through my mind the day my dearest boyhood friend, George Bendall, came to tell me about the first time he had intimate contact with a young lady. We were about thirteen, and I was sick in bed at the time. He was so excited and he wanted to tell me about it in every detail. He didn't go to bed with her or anything, but they were fooling around. I just couldn't believe it. I was amazed, and a little embarrassed for him.

I wouldn't have thought of doing any of that stuff myself. Not at the time anyway. The fact is, I swallowed the "party line." I believed it, and you know, the funny thing is I still do. To this day the values I learned in De Molay and at the First Baptist Church have been a yardstick for my life. I've probably strayed a lot off the path, but back then people like Mr. Reno and Mrs. Draper and Dr. Campbell kept me straight.

They were the kind of people a kid could look up to. I didn't really know any of them very well; it was what they *stood* for that made a big impression on me. Sometimes when you're not too familiar with people they can do you more good than someone around you whose flaws and faults are laid bare. Then you can become disappointed and disillusioned.

Maybe if I had gotten close to them I would have discovered that Mr. Reno used to break wind or that Mrs. Draper was the kind who invited the iceman in for a drink and said, "Why don't you stick around awhile?"

Who knows? Who cares? The thing I remember about them is that they had so much love. There's a power in love that I swear is as strong as any transmitter sending out signals from radio or television or radar or laser beams.

Maybe I'm just a little more gullible than the next guy to have fallen for all of this. But the way I see it, somewhere along the line I've been given one of the greatest gifts in the world, and that is to be receptive and sensitive to the kind of love I found among those folks at the First Baptist Church.

So to me the miracle in all this is in the timing. Dr. Campbell and his crowd came into my life at a time when I was ready to receive their signals. And timing was also crucial when a well-known radio correspondent inadvertently set me on the road to a career that was to become one of the lasting joys of my life.

CHAPTER 6

The Little Engine That Could

I was all set for a big time in the big city. My mother and I had gone into Washington on the old AB&W bus, and she had left me by myself at the Earle Theater to see a show while she went shopping.

For an eight-year-old that was heady stuff. In those days they had vaudeville shows there, with a real live pit orchestra and an organ that led the crowd in sing-alongs. And then you'd see a movie.

When the movie ended a little early, I decided to explore the building the theater was in. On one of the floors was WTOP radio, one of the big stations at the time. So I pushed the elevator button and rode up to see what it was all about.

I got off the elevator and without hesitating marched

right up to the reception desk. As luck would have it, the receptionist at the station took a shine to me. Maybe she felt sorry for this little kid all alone. Maybe I was cute and smiley. At any rate, she took me on a little tour, showing me the studios and how the station worked.

Then she took me back to one of the studios where a live broadcast was going on.

"If you're very quiet," she said, "you can sit here in the control room. The newsman in there just got back from Asia. He's a correspondent for CBS, and he bailed out of a plane that went down in the mountains of Burma. He was stranded for a month before he made it back to civilization. This is one of his first broadcasts back in the States."

I don't remember a word the man said. But after the show was over, the guy came out of the studio and started walking in my direction. He was tall and thin, and his face was kind of ruddy. The receptionist introduced me to Eric Sevareid.

He was my inspiration. As soon as I got home, I headed for the basement and began setting up a mock radio station from things I had lying around. I took three yo-yos, split them in half, and with a hammer and nail drove them into the handrail that went down to the basement. The yo-yos spun around like dials on a control panel.

For a microphone I took a soap dish, the kind that sticks into the wall in a men's room and holds a round receptacle. When I took out the soap dish, what I had left was a circle in a stand. I strung strings across it to make a "pretend" microphone.

With my yo-yo control panel and soap-dish mike, I was ready to go on the air. From that time on, radio became an obsession. It was just a hobby, but I worked at it day and night. That's all I thought about and all I wanted to do with my life.

One thing about me, when I get involved in something, I will stick to it, often to the point of being bull-headed about it. There are very few things I undertake to do that I don't think I can do. Like the Little Engine That Could, I tend to enjoy new challenges. Instead of being intimidated or put off by something that seems beyond my reach, I'll jump right in and try, and keep trying until I make it. I just don't give up easily.

I remember one time I was given a dog by one of my neighbors. He was a longhaired mutt with a collie look about him. I kept him in the backyard, but that darn dog would constantly jump out of the backyard and go to his old home. It was like he had a built-in radar system inside him that told him which way to go. So I called him Radar.

Every time he jumped out and tried to run away, I'd chase after him and put him in the basement. But the minute he was in the backyard again, that dog would head for his former home, running like a bat out of hell, with his tail straight out and his ears flapping. And out I'd go, chasing him back.

It went on like that for a couple of weeks. Then one day I finally just got fed up with the whole thing. I started out to chase him, but then just turned on my heels and started walking back home. And wouldn't you know, that dog turned around and followed me. As soon as I stopped chasing him, he came home.

I was so happy to see him. And I remember thinking that once you give something its proper effort—I had tried and tried with that dog—nine times out of ten you'll succeed in what you set out to do.

As an eight-year-old kid I was just as persistent about radio. I got a bunch of the neighborhood kids together and we formed a radio club. Our big project was setting up a real radio station in my basement, using a phono oscillator I bought. It was actually a record player with a miniature transmitter and it came in at a certain spot on the radio dial. It was a wireless phonograph. We added a microphone to it, played records into the microphone, and started "broadcasting" from my house. Our "station" had a range of maybe a hundred yards in either direction.

We called the station WSSD. It stood for Willard Scott, then a guy named Sharp, and a kid named Derek Adams. Then there was Jimmy Rudin, who is now a well-known rabbi in New York, and Roger Gordon, who went on to become an expert in audiovisual techniques. At one point Roger got a little more ambitious and bought a souped-up phono oscillator through a catalog. His had a range of about five miles. The problem was that his house was near National Airport, and his "broadcasts" were coming in over Pan American's communications channel every Saturday morning. One day we were at his house when a man from the FCC came by to close down his station.

But our little station in my basement didn't have such problems, and all of us kids got together after school and all day Saturday to do our broadcasts. We had such provocative programs as "Rudin's Portfolio"—fifteen minutes of in-depth comments on Harry Truman or the Marshall Plan. He was the Edward R. Murrow of the pimple set.

I was the disc jockey. But my big thing, always, was to be an announcer. I would listen to the announcers on radio over and over again and mimic the way they modulated their voices. Pretty soon I had it down pat.

As I said, I always did things whole hog, and our station even carried commercials. We sold spots to the local drugstore, beauty shop, and grocery store at a quarter apiece. Nobody heard them except Mr. Vance next door—but he listened to us.

All my life I've always made money. In fact I can never remember when I didn't hustle a buck. As a kid I had two paper routes instead of one. For about three or four years there I sold the *Washington Post*, the *Times-Herald*, and the *Alexandria Gazette*.

During the war, we put on shows in the basement and sold tickets to the kids in the neighborhood. I had a 16mm Keystone projector and one or two newsreels of battleships which I'd show. Then we'd reenact some bits from Irving Berlin's *This Is the Army*, which was a big hit on Broadway. We did ad libs and little plots and sang. One of the songs was "This Is the Army, Mr. Jones," another was "Oh How I Hate to Get Up in the Morning."

All the kids in the neighborhood came and we made four or five bucks from it. It was a big summertime project. With the money I made, I bought stamps for a savings bond. That was my "war effort." I was a patriotic little devil!

Even as a kid I was a dynamite salesman. For a while I sold magazines—*Reader's Digest, Life*—and I always sold more than anybody. I was just persistent. And I was never afraid to ask anyone. There's a difference between being pushy and being enthusiastic about what you do. That's how I sold magazines, with lots of genuine enthusiasm. If my mother was having a bridge party, for example, I'd go up to all her girl friends and sell two or three subscriptions.

A lot of my motivation for all this hustling was to make money to buy things for the radio station. When I wasn't busy making money for the station, I was out doing things that gave me more exposure to broadcasting, but not out of any calculated move to get experience for a career. I simply loved doing it. The same motivation guides me today. I just enjoy doing what I do.

I was the kind of kid who was always chosen to run the projector in school. You know, those fifteen-minute films that showed how grasshoppers mated. The teacher always picked me and I ate it up. I set up the screen, ran the projector, and got the biggest kick out of it.

Once I got Herman to take me to the Reed Theater in Alexandria to see the projection room. He talked to the guy who ran the place and got permission for me to watch the projectionist work. That was one of the highlights of my life. The movie that day was *Road to Morocco*, and I saw it from up in the projection room overlooking the theater. The film was the old 35 mm, huge stuff, about two inches wide. In those days they used huge arc lamps, like those the coal miners wore on their heads, to project the film on the screen. And nothing was automated. The projectionist had to do everything.

By the time I reached high school, all this fooling around with radio, and that relentless hustler's drive I had, started to pay off as I moved into the "big time."

The big time for me back then was WPIK in Alexandria. On Friday nights, my buddy George Bendall and I would pay a visit to the station, which was in the George Mason Hotel. That was a big deal. We'd go down to WPIK, then go to Whelan's drugstore for a soda, and then come home about eleven. That was our version of a Friday night rumble.

The first time we went down to the station, we peeked through the window of the studio and there was a guy named Howard Severe playing one of Benny Goodman's records. It was a big benchmark in my life, like the time I heard George describe his first time making out with a girl. I thought to myself, if I could ever do what Howard's doing, I'd be in fat city.

George and I got to be regulars down at WPIK on Friday nights, and we would just hang around, watching Howard spin the discs and listening to the announcer, a young guy from Kansas City named Dave Widder. One night when we were hanging around, Dave let me make a station break. I was really scared. I had to say "WPIK Alexandria." It was the first time I had been on the air commercially.

That just whetted my appetite for more. Later on, I talked Dave Widder into doing a high school show and he found some old radio scripts called "Lady Make Believe." They were nothing more than a bunch of stories like "Jack and the Beanstalk," featuring a heroine named Lady Make Believe. But these scripts were enough to get our imaginations spinning.

The show was broadcast live every Saturday with me as the announcer, a professional actress as Lady Make Believe, and a cast of thirteen or fourteen kids, all volunteers from local high schools, whom we could draw upon for various characters. We rehearsed Fridays after school.

But what really sold the show was a gimmick we dreamed up for audience participation. We formed a high school radio club and had listeners send in drawings of what they thought Lady Make Believe looked like. We got four hundred letters a week, all loyal fans. The show took off. And so did my radio career.

A few weeks after Lady Make Believe got started, I

had the chance to audition for a fifteen-minute high school news program that was being started by WCFM. One of my teachers, Mrs. Edwina Parker, an attractive woman who looked like Evita, suggested I audition on behalf of George Washington High School. About twenty of us from high schools around the District competed for the announcer's job, and I got it. The show was on the air every Saturday night. In those days not too many people had FM sets, so my parents had to go over to a neighbor's house to listen.

After my show was over, I'd hang around the station to see what was what. And you know the old bit about hanging around: "you are who you hang around with." From my experience, I would say, if you really want to get into radio or television, just hang around. In my case, the show that followed was a music program called *Saturday Night Dancing Party*, and a couple of times the disc jockeys didn't show up. After about six months, I showed I was dependable, so they gave me the show.

I was a disc jockey. From eight to midnight I played music of bands that recorded specialized music for "transcriptions." These were like big phonograph records, about 16 inches in diameter, that had 15 minutes on either side. They ran at 33⅓ but with a 78 needle. I'd come in every 15 minutes and say, "You've just heard . . . ," or "You're about to hear. . . ." Then I'd read the news and do the weather.

So here I was, all of about thirteen or fourteen years old, barely out of short pants and already juggling three weekly radio shows. Of course I didn't get paid for any of this stuff, but who cared! I just kept plugging away, doing what I loved doing, purely for the fun of it. Once I had my foot in the door of professional radio there was no stopping me.

My mind was always thinking of new gimmicks for radio programs. My buddy Roger Gordon and I came up with a concept for a radio show called *High School Hit Parade*. The idea was to spin the top ten records of the week chosen by *Billboard* or *Variety*, and intersperse the music with chatter from Roger and me aimed at the teenage audience in the District. We wanted to get the kids involved by holding contests and giving away prizes.

We were all fired up by the idea. After all, we had had all those years of experience in my basement and I was now a "pro." We were sure that the folks at WOL radio would be falling all over themselves with enthusiasm.

So Roger and I marched over to WOL to meet with the program director. We ended up going over there five or six times, like a couple of Little Engines That Could. Every time we went, the program director was always very nice to us, but he kept putting us off. Finally, he gave in and said that we'd have to take it up with the station owner who was coming to town a few days later. But he left it at that, and still nothing happened.

But we didn't leave it there. We found out where the big muckety-muck was staying and we camped outside his hotel room door until he came out. He had checked in around four and when he emerged around eight or nine o'clock to go out for a drink, there we were, right smack on his doorstep.

Needless to say, he was stunned. He certainly didn't want to stand there in the hallway discussing our big idea about a High School Hit Parade. But he was impressed enough by our persistence that he gave us an appointment. "If you come by the office tomorrow we'll talk about it," he said.

We went to his office, and he gave us the show. Just like that. But the fact is, it hadn't just fallen into our laps. It didn't just happen. We were enthusiastic about it. We pursued it. And as a result, as mere teenagers we ended up with a weekly show on a major Washington, D.C., station that opened up doors to the big time.

Frank Blair was our announcer. He did the news before our show and then he'd say "High School Hit Parade is brought to you by the public schools in the District and Maryland and Virginia. And here are your hosts, Willard Scott and Roger Gordon."

Frank, of course, later became a staff announcer at WRC, which was the NBC affiliate in Washington. From there he went to the *Today Show* in New York.

I soon followed Frank to WRC, but not because of "pull." Again, it was persistence and pluck that saw me through.

I had wanted to be a page at WRC ever since my radio club days. Derek Adams' mom had taken us there when I was about ten years old, and I never forgot the experience. We saw a show called "Wonder Flame of the Air" put on by the Washington Gas Company. They had a twelve-to-fourteen piece orchestra; it was a big extravaganza. As we watched the show being put together, I was gaga. What impressed me as much as seeing the show being assembled was the building it was in. The station was in the Trans-Lux building, a fabulous art deco design with funny lettering and weird-looking clocks.

But I especially remember seeing all these young kids rushing back and forth in uniforms with the NBC insignia on them. And I made up my mind right then that someday I'd be wearing one of those uniforms too. I knew that you had to be a certain age to be a page, so I waited until I was sixteen, and then I went for an interview.

The personnel director was a lady named Eleanor Ferguson, and again I lucked out. She was a lovely lady, really nice and kind, and she told me that the first time they had a job opening on weekends she'd be in touch.

But I didn't wait for her to call back. Every week I bugged them and bugged them. Finally, she called to say that someone was sick and they needed a part-time page the next weekend. It was a one-shot deal, she said, but if I worked out all right she'd let me be a regular substitute.

My first day on the job was Saturday, September 16, 1950. I was sixteen years old, and I felt like a million bucks. But I was also scared stiff. I remember going over to Epiphany Episcopal Church on G street and saying a prayer. I wanted that job so badly that I knew I needed some big help. I had never encountered the relative formality of an Episcopal church before, and going off the street into one in Washington, D.C., was quite an experience for me—on the order of going into the Vatican.

I walked into that little church, kneeled, and said, "Please God, I'd like to have that job."

A week later, I was called back to work as a regular "utility hitter" on Friday nights, Saturday mornings, and Sundays. Eventually I ended up working regularly on weekends.

As a page, I was basically a go-fer. The job started in the morning at eight o'clock and the first thing you did was get coffee and hot dogs at Howard Johnson's across the street and bring them over for everybody. Then you'd go down to the corner and pick up coffee and

Danish and things like that at People's Drugstore. Then maybe I'd work the switchboard and sort and deliver the mail. In the afternoon, I ran football scores to the announcer on duty.

I had a uniform: a coat and pants, navy blue with a little NBC emblem showing a fire coming out of the microphone. I still have that uniform somewhere.

It may not have seemed like much, getting coffee and working switchboards or whatever. But the air was always crackling with excitement, particularly on Sundays when we broadcast Theodore Granik's old radio show, *American Forum of the Air*. He had a list of famous guests who paraded through the studio leaving us all star-struck. At NBC in those days, there was always somebody famous popping in: Elizabeth Taylor at age twenty, Spencer Tracy, Secretary of State Dean Acheson and Eleanor Roosevelt. One of the highlights of my paging career was the day the elevator door opened and Trigger, Roy Rogers, Dale Evans and Billy Graham walked out.

The closest I got to anyone, though, was to Eleanor Roosevelt. Actually, it was her coat I was close to. She had this very famous coat, a half-length caracul. It was kind of her trademark—she wore it everywhere.

She came in to do *American Forum of the Air* and asked me to take good care of her coat for her. I didn't want to hang it in the lobby where all the other coats were, so I took it into the office of our vice president, Scoop Russell, and put it in his closet. Then I went about my business, and eventually took off for lunch.

When Mrs. Roosevelt came out of the studio, she couldn't find her coat and she couldn't find me. I'm sure she was fit to be tied since, as I said, the coat was kind of a trademark with her. Somehow or other she found something to wear to the Press Club a few blocks away where she went for a luncheon.

When I got back from my lunch, I learned about the "missing coat." So, in a near-panic I ran it down to the Press Club and sheepishly handed it to her.

She wasn't exactly nasty. But she wasn't thrilled either.

But not even Eleanor Roosevelt could dampen my spirits about my job. I was crazy about it. You know how guys write their girls' names on their notebooks? Well, even as crazy as I was about my old girl friend, Barbara Hubbard, instead of writing her name on my notebook I'd write WRC and NBC.

All I ever wanted out of life was to be a radio announcer for NBC. I wanted to make $250 a week and come off the AB&W bus with the *Evening Star* rolled under my arm like Mr. Julian Davis, a neighbor who worked for the Southern Railroad.

But I knew I could never be an announcer until I had more experience. So I started looking for more radio jobs in my free time. At this point I was juggling my weekend page's job at WRC with my stints as an announcer for *High School Hit Parade* on Saturday morning and WCFM's *Dancing Party* at night.

An announcing job didn't come through right away. But one of the disc jockeys at WRC, Jerry Strong, had another job at WINX and he arranged for me to work in the music library during the summer. The station was in a pretty tacky part of Washington, right across from a whorehouse, and my job was little more than that of a file clerk. But I was willing to put up with almost anything.

I used to pass the time by looking out the window, and every two weeks or so the cops would raid the whorehouse. I'd call people in the building and say, "Hey, it's happening," and everyone would come running down to watch the action.

As you may have gathered by now, I was working with a vengeance at all of these jobs. Most people think that everything I have has been handed to me. But actually it's been a concentrated effort. It's not really work because it's fun. But I've been hustling and "stick-to-it-ing" every step of the way. I've stuck to it all through thick and thin.

Under normal conditions, someone who had the *High School Hit Parade* might have said, "I'm not going to come back at night to do the FM recording job," or "I'm not going to be a page because I'm on the air—why should I be delivering mail and coffee to somebody when I've got my own radio show?"

But that wasn't me. The way I looked at it, even back then, was that *90 percent of anything is being there.* And it was because I was there, as a page at WRC, that I finally got my big break. The station agreed to give me an audition for the job of summer relief announcer. It was a token audition; they were only letting me do it to be nice to me. About twenty guys auditioned for two openings they had that summer of 1953. Two of them were hired, and I wasn't one of them.

But about a month after the summer relief jobs were filled, one of the guys picked up and left because his wife hated living in Washington. So now they had an opening. By now, though, everybody else who had taken the audition had gotten work elsewhere. The only person left whom they could use was me. I was still at the station, doing my paging job.

"Give it to the kid," they said.

Two months later Frank Blair went to the *Today Show*

in New York and they needed somebody to replace Frank as the regular announcer. Again, *I was there.* They knew me and liked me and I had proven myself. So they hired me. I was just nineteen, the second youngest staff announcer ever hired by NBC.

CHAPTER 7

Let Your Conscience
Be Your Guide

I'm a sucker for a good cause. When something comes along that stirs my passions, I'll get behind it 100 percent, no matter what the consequences.

That may sound foolhardy, or even stupid. But there's nothing like the feeling you get when you stick your neck out for a person or a principle that's important to you. When you take a stand *for* something, the juices start flowing and you get consumed by a joyful energy that spills over into everything you do.

I like to fancy myself as Cyrano de Bergerac, that swashbuckling hero of French drama who was a symbol of courage, independence, and self-sacrifice. You may remember him as the guy with the big nose who was quick with a sword and with a line of poetry.

What always appealed to me about Cyrano was that he never went along with the crowd. He wasn't big on fancy manners or fancy clothes or fancy friends. What mattered to him was being true to his ideals, even at the risk of making enemies. A well-connected count named De Guiche, for example, suggested that Cyrano could make a few bucks on his poetry and win some important friends by making a little compromise and changing a few lines. This didn't sit at all well with our hero, who rather ungraciously told the guy he was all wet.

Cyrano had no apologies for his behavior: "There are things in this world a man does well to carry to extremes," he told his buddies. Cyrano stood for something. He was willing to risk life, limb, and even his reputation for his principles.

One thing he couldn't stomach was a bully, and he was quick to come to the rescue of the weak and defenseless. When he heard that a friend was about to be ambushed, he deliberately traded places with the guy and set himself up as the target. Then he single-handedly made mincemeat of one hundred swordsmen who had been lying in wait for his friend.

That's what I call macho!

Cyrano may have been a sucker, but in a funny way he was happy pursuing his heroic ideals. It all goes back to that old cornball line of Shakespeare's "To thine own self be true." Cyrano was true to himself, and in the end he went out in style.

I can understand how he felt. There have been a few moments in my life when I've had to put myself on the line for something I believed in. At those times I've felt darn proud of myself for doing what I knew was right. Now I can't claim that I get worked up over every injustice known to man. But there are two principles that

I've been downright bullheaded about since I was a kid.

Principle #1: Support the underdog. I've always had a soft spot for the little guy. When I was about ten, I befriended some bums who gathered by the railroad tracks near my home. There was a creek behind our row of houses, and behind that a patch of woods and then the railroad tracks. A lot of hoboes who were riding the rails would get off at Alexandria and sleep in the woods in cardboard boxes.

I'd go over and talk to them because, to me, they weren't social misfits. They were nice—no dirty words—just nice folks. I was fascinated by their old raggedy clothes and their tales of where they had been and where they were going. My heart went out to them. I'd run home and slice some Velveeta cheese and put it on Wonder bread smeared with mayonnaise, and then I'd bring them sandwiches so they'd have something to eat.

Why I didn't get killed or molested I'll never know. Maybe they sensed that I sympathized with them, or maybe I was just lucky.

In school, too, I was always drawn to the kids who didn't quite fit in. When somebody new came into class, I would run over and make friends with him, instead of making fun of him as an outsider. My earliest act of heroism in that regard came in the boys' room in third grade.

George Bendall had just come from Cleveland. He was a big gawky kid, and I got wind of the fact that some of the other kids were going to gang up on George and try to beat him up in the men's room.

I had always hated gangs. You know how when kids band together sometimes the worst in them comes out.

The sixth grade used to beat up the fifth-graders and so forth. They got me one time and gave me a "pink belly." That's when they take off your shirt, spit on your stomach, cover it with sand, and then rub the sand into your stomach. The one kid who did that to me I finally kicked.

But back to George. Here he was, about to be ambushed, like Cyrano's pal who faced the hundred swordsmen. I remember watching as he went into the boys' room and a bunch of guys went in after him. George was big enough that he could probably have sat on them. But I went to his rescue anyway.

"If you're going to beat him up, you'll have to take me too," I said boldly. To me it was injustice, and I had a choice. I could be frightened, or I could be magnificent. That time I was magnificent, and the bullies backed down.

Principle #2: Speak the truth. I'm a fanatic about the subject of honesty, almost as fanatic as Cyrano was about not compromising his principles. When I see something amiss, I just have to tell the truth, the whole truth, and nothing but the truth. It's like a compulsion. I *have* to open my mouth and throw in my two cents, even if no one wants to hear it.

My first big chance to put my money where my mouth was came in high school, when I ran for the presidency of the senior class. I came out against fraternities.

It was a suicide mission. I was all hung up on the fact that they wouldn't allow Jews in the fraternities, and I said so. It went against all my principles. I don't want or need the protection of a group. I'd never belong to a country club. I've never liked this collective socializing business—it tends to make for snobbery.

85

So, in my campaign I said straight out that public schools weren't the place for fraternities and there was no way I was going to put up with it.

You have to understand, though, that like Cyrano with his sword, I was operating from a certain position of strength and didn't have a whole lot to lose. I had been class president for three years running and was known all over town. My high visibility had something to do with the fact that when I was fifteen I had played George Washington in Alexandria's sesquicentennial play *Alexandria Thy Sons*. That's like playing the part of the Pope at the Vatican, because Alexandria was George Washington's hometown.

At any rate, I played young George, the surveyor, and after that I was a hero. Everybody in town knew who I was because I was in all the papers. That theatrical success led to my being chosen as the only freshman in the senior class play. I played the part of a guy with an Italian accent. I was terrible, but I stood out because I was big. That role gave me a certain modicum of recognition, which got me the class presidency for the next three years. That's the way it was in high school. For better or for worse, I was the only one everybody knew so I got elected.

When I ran for reelection my senior year, it could have been clear sailing if I had kept my mouth shut. But as I said, I couldn't hold myself back from speaking out, even if it meant losing. Luckily, I won anyway—but by a narrow hair.

Once I discovered that telling the truth didn't necessarily hurt, I never shut up. In fact, I had so much to say about so many things that my father once told me, "Charlie, if B.S. were music, you'd be a one-man band."

Some people didn't mind the music. When I was a young kid at WRC in Washington, the general manager of the station, Carleton Smith, used to call me in to talk to him because he knew I wouldn't smooth things over. Most people on the staff were afraid even to go into his office. He had the reputation of being responsible for the firing of Arthur Godfrey and of working for a while as a presidential announcer for Franklin Roosevelt.

Short and stocky, with a huge voice, Smith had the bearing of a fine, aristocratic Southern gentleman. Nothing crude ever came out of him. He was so classy that when he came to work in the morning, his cuff links were a quarter of an inch below his coat sleeve, and when he left at precisely 5:30 they were still a quarter of an inch below his sleeve. All this spit and polish made him a bit unapproachable, and no one dared speak to him except to say "How are you, sir?"

No one, of course, except me. He had something against Mario Lanza. He hated him. It would have been the easiest thing in the world for us not to play Mario Lanza on our programs. But I remember telling him straight out, "Mario Lanza's the hottest thing going. Why should you inflict your personal opinions on a radio station just because you happen to be the manager?"

My heart was skipping beats as I told him what was on my mind. He didn't say anything. He just held up his hand in a gesture of blessing as if to say "Thank you."

I don't remember whether he took my advice. But I do remember that instead of holding it against me, he got behind me.

Even in the Navy as a lowly seaman a few years later, I couldn't put a clamp on my mouth. Most of my two-year career in the Navy was spent doing a radio show in Norfolk, Virginia, called *Dateline NATO*. For one particular show, the admiral's wife taped a broadcast on a cookbook the NATO women had put together. During the taping, she kept referring to the book's wonderful "receeps."

I knew she meant recipes, but I also knew that nobody listening would have the slightest idea what she was talking about. So I told her politely, "Perhaps there's another way of saying recipes that I'm not aware of. I'm just an average listener, and I'm not sure I'd understand what you were saying."

It turned out it was the English pronunciation. She said, "I'll be happy to do it again," and her program was a big success.

Now, I'll have to admit that I didn't come by these two principles, or any others for that matter, as a result of hard thinking. The fact is, what moves me is the sheer force of gut instinct. God has given me the greatest gift I have, and that's common sense. For the most part, I know instantly if something is right or not. The only time I've gone wrong in life is when I sat down and thought about something and tried to figure it out analytically. That method, which is sure to fail, I call "Willard Logic."

So instead of using "Willard Logic," I prefer to follow the uncomplicated reasoning of Jiminy Cricket who said, "Let your conscience be your guide."

One of the biggest joys I've gotten out of following my conscience is picking the right friends. The secret of my success is that I knew the kind of people to hang around with. I'm not talking about power and money and all that. I'm talking about people who had something to offer, who have added to my life.

When it comes to friends, there's no one I've been closer to and gained more from than a fellow I first met as a student at American University in Washington. If you didn't know better, it might have seemed that this guy got more from me than I got from him, because, you see, he was blind.

CHAPTER 8

The *Joy Boys*, or Lessons in How to Be a Sidekick

My friendship with Eddie Walker began with a weird sort of practical joke when I was a college freshman.

Eddie was nineteen, a sophomore at American University, and had been blind from birth. My buddy from the basement radio days, Roger Gordon, had met Eddie at school the year before, and together they had rebuilt the campus radio station. Roger couldn't stop talking about this blind friend of his, and when I arrived on campus he made sure we got together.

The night we met, Eddie was on the air in the middle of a live broadcast. Roger and I sneaked into the station, and Roger whispered to me, "Why don't you slip across the table and talk to him?"

I had never met the guy before in my life, but I was

game for anything. As quietly as I could, I tiptoed to a seat opposite Eddie and sat down. Eddie, of course, couldn't see a thing, and he was so absorbed doing his show that he didn't seem to know I was there.

When an opening came in his monologue, I started kidding around with him on the air. If I took him by surprise, he never showed it, because he never missed a beat.

From the moment he parried a response, I knew we were onto something. We were like one mind, one thought. We had an uncanny ability to second-guess each other, to read each other's thoughts. We were a natural team.

It didn't take long for Eddie and me to put our heads together for a radio show. I had contacts at the commercial station, WOL, where I had done *High School Hit Parade*, and so we talked them into giving us twenty-five minutes at eleven o'clock Sunday night for a comedy show.

It was called *Going AWOL*. We had a theme song called "Sicilian Tarantella" done by Henry Renee's orchestra. Then we played two or three records and did a few skits we had put together. One of our skits was a takeoff on the movie *Scaramouche*. We called it "Scratch a Pooch." For craziness like this, we got paid $25 a show.

The program was such a hit that the station soon put us on Saturday night from eight till midnight. It was more of the same, popular songs, skits. For some extra oomph, we added football scores. We had a window overlooking Connecticut Avenue, and I would sit in the window and read the football scores right off the ticker tape and wave to people. The cabs would honk back at us on the street below.

About a year after we started our show at WOL I got my big break as a staff announcer at WRC. That was in 1953, while I was a junior in college. I would go to school in the daytime and work as a staff announcer at night and between classes. That job also turned out to be a ticket to the top for Eddie and me. Carleton Smith, the manager of WRC, asked us to do a show five days a week at 7:05 P.M. So we jumped ship at WOL and began a comedy program on WRC that was to keep us together professionally for the next seventeen years.

We called ourselves the *Joy Boys*. We didn't get off to such a joyful start, though. Our show replaced the *Lone Ranger* and the *Longine Symphonette*, and the phone calls poured in with complaints.

But somehow, we won them over with such memorable skits as "Gums—the Story of an Old Shark." He had no teeth. He'd bite rubber rafts but couldn't do any damage to the metal boats. The *Joy Boys* had no music, nothing but comedy routines like this which we wrote ourselves. I was the idea man and did most of the writing. Eddie was an actor. He is a marvelous mimic.

Behind the scenes, Eddie was the one in control of the minute-to-minute broadcasts. You know the old saying: There are two types of people, those who like to work and those who like to watch. Well, when we did a radio show, Eddie did all the work—in braille. He would cue the engineer for the commercials, and give the time from a braille clock. He's a perfectionist, one of the most orderly, organized people I've ever known in my life, and a fanatic about details.

In contrast, I sort of let the chips fall where they may. People would say to me, "What the heck do you do?"

The fact of the matter was, Eddie *had* to be in charge behind the scenes. If I had been running the show, it would have been necessary to find some way to communicate with him. I could have hit him or punched him or something to give him his cues. But he wanted to be in control, and so I stepped back willingly and enjoyed my role as his sidekick.

The station liked what we did so much that a year after we started they put us on during the popular "drive time" from four to six.

The magic in the *Joy Boys* was that the two of us loved each other. Damon and Pythias never knew friendship like ours. We operated together more closely than most people do when they are married, and yet we never had a fight, we never had an argument. We never even had a contract. Our bond was our word. We were like blood brothers, and still are after almost thirty years.

From the moment we met over that live mike in college, we were inseparable. We constantly had our heads together doing some project or other. Once we teamed up to buy a car. We happened to walk by a raunchy used-car lot and saw a '38 Plymouth in the lot. It was green, four-door, and it turned out it had gone through World War II. It looked like it had gone through the front lines. The guy wanted $75 for it.

"If it only runs a block," he said, "it's a good buy."

Sure enough, it only ran a block. We ended up having to push it back to the lot. Because Eddie couldn't see, I ended up driving and he ended up pushing.

You might say it was a case of the blind leading the blind. We carried that theme one step further a couple of years later when we got drunk as skunks and went riding along the freeway in my baby blue '53 Pontiac convertible.

"I wish I could drive," said Eddie.

"What makes you think you can't?" I said. With that,

I put him in the driver's seat and started giving him directions. "A little more to the right, Eddie," I'd say. Or, "We're coming to the light. Put your foot on the brake."

Here he was, blind as a bat, driving down the freeway for two miles, with me hooting and hollering at his side. That's the way it went with me and Eddie.

We used to double-date all the time, and when he was dating his wife up in Maryland, I'd sit and wait in the car until he was ready to go home. Sometimes he got me dates with a girl who was blind. We were just good friends. We'd sit in the car and wait for Eddie to get off the porch.

In those days, the most risqué thing that anybody did was touch. That's about it. You were afraid to do much back then because nobody wanted to get anybody pregnant.

At any rate, Eddie would be up there on the porch all hot and heavy, and I'd be in the car with this blind girl listening to the radio and telling her jokes. When he was ready to go, I'd drive him home.

Our teamwork also carried over into the classroom. He had a portable braille-writer and an old stylus that he took notes with. The thing looked like a carrot shredder, and it made a heck of a racket. We'd be sitting in English class, with everyone half asleep and the professor babbling on, and Eddie would be working this machine. I finally said to him, "Why do that? I'll take notes and read them to you during breaks in our radio show and you can put it on tape."

The irony was that using my notes, Eddie got a B in the course and I got a D. He was smart as they come—his whole family was smart—and he sailed through school.

I was always a rotten student. In grade school I got

C's and B's, in high school I had dropped to C's and D's, and by the time I got to college, it was getting almost disastrous. I got the lowest grade in the history of American University on a French test. I scored a 12. The teacher just recommended that before I do myself any harm I get out.

In geology it was more of the same. I loved my geology teacher, and I was fascinated by the subject. I even bought a mineral book and would go out and hunt for things. But when it came to the tests, I couldn't pull it all together. The teacher should have failed me, but he gave me straight D's because he knew I liked the stuff so much.

Outside school I was already becoming a success professionally. As I said, when I was a junior I landed the job as staff announcer at WRC and was making $12,000 a year, more than most of the professors. But inside school, by my senior year my academic career looked doomed.

What saved me was the dean of men, John E. Bentley. He was a Scotsman who had gone to McGill University in Canada. He called me into the office one day, and said, "Oh, you poor son of a bitch, you're not going to make it. You're going to flunk out."

"What can I do?" I asked.

"You take one of my courses." I did, and I got through.

Dean Bentley may have been the one who helped me graduate from college, but when it came to the lasting lessons of life, it was Eddie Walker who, as the saying goes, taught me everything I know. People used to say to me, "Oh, aren't you nice, helping that blind guy." But the truth is, Eddie was the one who helped *me*, in ways that nobody but a person like him could help.

In the first place, Eddie taught me to be thankful for

what I have. You can't be around someone like Eddie very long and keep taking your own life for granted. It's like an old line from the Baptist devotional book *Open Windows*: "An ungrateful man is like a hog eating acorns under an oak tree. He never looks up to see where they came from."

If I ever felt sorry for myself, I couldn't stay that way for long watching Eddie operate. He was the original positive thinker, who turned every obstacle to advantage. Typical was the way he turned an operation to remove his eyes into an asset. He had been blind from birth because of a problem with the optic nerve. Later it gave him terrible headaches, and eventually he got glaucoma and had to have his eyes removed.

When the guy asked him what color glass he wanted in his eye sockets, brown or blue, Eddie said, "I'll take a pair of each."

He switched eyes depending on the tie. One day he made a mistake and came in with one blue eye and one brown one.

Like Eddie, most of the blind people I've met over the years have had a great attitude toward life. Unfortunately, people tend to lump blindness with other handicaps. They think if you're blind you're also either deaf or have mental problems. There was even a home for the blind in Washington once called "The Washington Home for the Incurables." Can you imagine being sent there? They would have been more accurate calling it "Home for the Happies."

Blind people tend to make the most of the abilities they do have. They are extra sharp in their hearing and extra sharp in their other senses, like bats. Eddie could walk down a hall and tell where to turn into a doorway. He said the click of his heels would echo off the wall and act like radar, and he could tell the different changes when he came to a door or opening.

Along with helping me count my blessings, my friendship with Eddie also taught me to look for the basic goodness in everybody. Eddie always brought out the very best in people. He needs to have basic things done for him, and people have always been quick to meet those needs. Particularly in college, someone was always there helping him cross the street, offering to take him down to the store to get a haircut, cutting his meat at the table, or getting him a second helping.

What's more, the help was always given with enthusiasm and eagerness. I see time and time again with Eddie that people are just waiting, like a door to be opened, to pour out all this love. All they need is the chance.

My friendship with Eddie, who was and is my closest confidant, also showed me the value of trusting another human being with my innermost secrets. Millions of people have no one they can talk over problems with, either because they're too embarrassed or they don't think anybody's interested.

But with Eddie, I always had someone I could open up to. To this day there's nothing about my life he doesn't know. Maybe he doesn't care as much as I think he does, and maybe he cares more. But the point is I can share with him, honestly.

The Catholic Church has a thing called confession, and believe me, they've got a good thing going. Over the years of confessing my foibles and fears to Eddie, I've found that there's tremendous benefit in letting it all hang out with a friend. It's almost a religious experience.

Perhaps the most important lesson I learned from

Eddie, though, was humility—how to graciously stand back and let someone else take the limelight, at least for a little while.

Every time Eddie and I walked into a room, people made a beeline for him and started to make a fuss. They'd fall all over themselves to be the ones who got him a drink or brought him a plate from the buffet. I was left on the sidelines to fend for myself.

Although we were equals on the air, even that took a certain amount of humility to carry off. We didn't have a straight man in our comedy routines. We just played to each other, alternating roles and pacing ourselves so that neither one of us hogged the act.

Like a horse, I learned when to brake and when to hold back so I didn't run away with the show. Left to myself, I could come on so strong that I could drive even our most loyal supporters nuts. As we used to joke in our comedy routines, the only real handicap Eddie ever had was me!

I have to admit that it didn't come naturally for me to rein in my ego. I disciplined myself to subordinate myself during nearly two decades of doing the *Joy Boys*. The reason that's so important to me now is that in the broadcasting business, everybody is totally wrapped up in himself, often to the detriment of the people he works with. My years with Eddie have helped me see myself in my proper role. I know what I can do, and I also know when I'll fall on my face.

Basically, I'm a team player. On TV the best foil for my routines would be a relatively serious anchorman because I'm the sidekick. He's Gene Autry, I'm Gabby Hayes. He's Roy Rogers, I'm Pat Brady—or Trigger. I come in and add the right touches.

On the *Today Show*, I'm the Gabby Hayes character.

Tom Brokaw was the cowboy in the hundred-dollar shirt, and I'm over there chewing tobacco and watching him kiss Jane Pauley.

I've always considered myself a Grade-B actor, a character actor. They're the ones you see in 1937 movies, and they're also the ones you see all the time on the Johnny Carson show and doing commercials. I prefer that because they will last for forty years. A star will either die, drink himself to death, or get so overexposed that people will get sick of him.

So, instead of going for the Clark Gable role, I'd rather be in the supporting cast. I'm not looking for easy fame, easy fortune, and easy friends. When I invest my time in something, I do it for keeps. Maybe that's one reason why my friendship with Eddie has lasted, and why, after more than thirty years, I'm still with NBC.

CHAPTER 9

God, Country, and NBC

I owe a lot in my life to looking up. One of the things I always looked up to was NBC and the man who built it, General David Sarnoff.

Of course, I never looked up to him physically: He was only about five feet four. But I was never really aware he was a little guy because he was such a dynamo. A feisty White Russian Jew who came over to the United States penniless in 1900, Sarnoff typified the whole up-by-your-bootstraps bit. He first gained recognition on April 14, 1912, the day the *Titanic* struck an iceberg, when he picked up an SOS at the telegraph station he was operating out on the top of the Wanamaker department store in New York City. At the time, the twenty-one-year-old Sarnoff worked for the Marconi Company. They later joined with General Electric to form a separate company called the Radio Corporation of America, RCA.

It was the old man, Sarnoff, though, who really built the RCA empire. During the war, Roosevelt made him a brigadier general and the label stuck, in part because that was how he ran RCA. It was a one-man company. When he wanted something done, he would just snap his fingers. But it wasn't an oppressive dictatorship. You *wanted* to do things for him. Still, he had a presence about him that demanded obedience.

The first contact I had with him was when I sent him the first dollar I ever made as a page at NBC. He signed it, and so did Arthur Godfrey.

Ten years later, during the Kennedy election, I was working in the studio in Washington as a staff announcer doing station breaks when an entourage walked by. I recognized our general manager and automatically stood up. The next thing I knew, he was saying to an erect little man in the center of the crowd, "This is Willard Scott, he's our announcer on duty."

And there stood my idol. Sarnoff came up to me and I stuck my hand out.

"Meeting you is one of the great moments of my career, General," I said. "You probably don't remember, but I sent you a dollar a few years back and you were nice enough to sign it."

"Where's the dollar now?" he asked.

"It's on the wall at home" I answered proudly.

"You're losing interest," he said. Then he crisply turned on his heels and walked out.

That's the way Sarnoff was. He never settled for less than he could get out of his company or out of the people who worked for him. He surrounded himself with the best, and the old NBC organization was a monument to his taste and style. It was, in a word, classy.

I've never considered myself classy, maybe that's why I was drawn to Sarnoff and NBC. All my life I've never wanted anything to do with number two. Number two is "poo-poo." Ever since I was a kid it's been poo-poo. I'm not obsessed with power: I just don't like the idea of being a loser. And when I started out with NBC under General Sarnoff, the company was a winner.

Sarnoff's management style at NBC was to promote from within. It was a feudal system. The top-ranked people were all prep school and Ivy League. At the bottom of the ladder were the pages. But as a page, you weren't considered a peon. Everyone knew you were there because you wanted to be in broadcasting. The idea was that you were kind of an acolyte entering a noble calling.

They gave you a year as a page, and in that year you saw every phase of the broadcasting business. If you didn't progress in that time, they just booted you out. A lot of things were taken into consideration. They looked at your initiative, the way you dressed. Everybody who wanted to make it big in broadcasting started out as a page: Dave Garroway, Gordon MacRae, Eva Marie Saint, Efrem Zimbalist, Jr., Tex Antoine, Bob Keeshan, David Hartman, and Ray Timothy, now president of the NBC Television Network. Once you passed muster you were in the NBC family. It was a tight-knit organization.

In those days, NBC was where the action was on every front in broadcasting. Washington, D.C., where I worked as a staff announcer, was the news center, and it was filled with the rising stars in the news world. The

NBC news show was called the *Camel News Caravan,* with John Cameron Swayze. He was the original news-man on television. One of the hot young Washington correspondents starting out on his show was a guy named David Brinkley. The local news director was Julian Goodman, who later became president of NBC news.

When it came to culture, NBC was making news. NBC commissioned Gian-Carlo Menotti to write *Amahl and the Night Visitors,* the first opera ever written for television. Before World War II, General Sarnoff had brought Toscanini over from Italy to form the first na-tional radio symphony, the NBC Symphony Orchestra.

Scientifically, NBC was at the cutting edge of televi-sion technology, and in the 1950s that meant color TV. CBS had developed a mechanical color-wheel system that did not show up on a black and white TV without an adapter. RCA created something called an all-elec-tronic compatible color system that could be received without color on existing black and white sets, or in color on special color sets. Eventually, the RCA system won out, and that's the one we watch today.

All of the RCA demonstration models were in Wash-ington, and when I was a page, I was assigned to work with them. I saw some of the first color pictures ever transmitted. They used various colored birds in cages, and they had a silly old Hammond organ for back-ground music. To show the different colors, the camera showed pictures of these birds twittering. *That* was color television.

My role in the development of color TV was what I call "mustard and moral support." I was assigned to pick up the hot dogs. I went to Howard Johnson's and got twenty-four hot dogs for the rest of the staff. But, like the deck boy on the *Santa Maria*, I was there, a minor participant but still present for history in the making.

I wouldn't have left the NBC family for anything. After all, I was there during a time of dramatic movement, I loved everything NBC and Sarnoff stood for. I was a staff announcer and my job gave me everything I wanted out of life. So as I say, I wouldn't have left for anything—anything, that is, except Uncle Sam.

Those were the days when the country still had compulsory military training, so I knew at some point I'd have to sign up. But I didn't want to be drafted into the Army like a mere pawn. I wanted to be able to say "I did it." So, I decided to join the Navy before the Army got me and thereby keep at least a little control over my own fate.

I enlisted on Seventeenth Street in Washington, D.C., right after Thanksgiving. It was November 26, 1956, and the city was just beginning to set up for the inauguration of President Eisenhower.

Herman took me over to the recruiting center and then walked me to the bus that would take me to basic training. It was an emotional moment for both of us, because I had never left home before. Here I was, twenty-two years old, a professional radio announcer, and I had never even been away from my folks.

I had the lowly title Seaman Recruit, and I was headed for boot camp in Bainbridge, Maryland. The base was on the Susquehanna River, only about thirty miles from my grandfather's farm. Most of the kids in boot camp with me were much younger and they were a rough bunch. They were so rough, in fact, that they forced a change of commanding officers. The first guy was too weak to handle them.

We ended up with a crusty, or as we say, "salty," guy named Benny Barkas, a Navy Chief who had been at Pearl Harbor. He had been on the *Arizona*, and when the ship blew up, he was blown out into the water and was given up for dead. The Navy found him, about three days after the attack, in a hospital in the boondocks. By that time, though, his family had already been notified of his demise. It turned out that Barkas had been injured and had floated around on a piece of wreckage until he was spotted by some Hawaiians who took him to a local clinic. The hospital was so primitive that nobody thought to let the Navy know they had found him.

Barkas was a heck of a guy, tough but oh so gentle. I actually saw him put a guy through a wall once in a nice way. These rough kids in our outfit—some of them were from New York gangs—had driven the other CO nuts. Then Barkas came in and it was the old John Wayne bit. He took this one wise guy by the collar, made a fist and knocked him through a wall. But when the kid recovered, Barkas treated him fairly, like everyone else, as though nothing had happened. The kid later turned out to be one of the best that ever graduated from Bainbridge. He even shook Barkas' hand when he left. Because of Barkas, my battalion, which had almost gotten court-martialed before he took over, ended up winning the battalion flag when we graduated.

Since I was older than the rest of the guys in boot camp, Barkas and I became good friends. We had a real racket going. He knew I didn't want to hang around the whole eight weeks, so from time to time he'd put me in the trunk of his car and take me through the Marine guard. We'd go off to town for a night out together.

Once, I told Barkas I wanted to get some underwear

and he even arranged for that. The Navy issues you boxer shorts, and I hated them. The horrible things drag down to your knees. I put up with them for the first few weeks, but then I told Barkas the problem. He packed me up in his car and took me to the dime store in Havre de Grace, Maryland, where you could get three pairs of jockey shorts for a buck.

I also managed to cozy up to some of the old chief petty officers and get out of guard duty. They made me battalion clerk. The real reason I got off guard duty, though, was my radio background. I was the only guy who knew how to catch the frequency of the *Grand Old Opry* for the chief who was on duty every Saturday night. To get it coming in clearly, I had to rig up a clothesline and some coat hangers and hook them to his radio. Sometimes it was almost impossible to find the signal, but one way or another I got the *Grand Old Opry* for him every Saturday night. Then we'd sit in this beat-up building we called the quarterdeck, listening to Minnie Pearl and drinking coffee.

When I finally got out of boot camp, I desperately wanted to go to sea. But somehow, every time I applied for sea duty, I ended up in some radio billet. That old theory that they find out what a man does and give him the opposite job didn't work with me. I did have one stint on shipboard, however. It was a two-week assignment to Guantanamo Bay, Cuba, as a "deck ape" on a destroyer, the *Robinson*, which had been through World War II. I swabbed the decks and shot a couple of guns during the cruise.

All this sailor-boy stuff was new to me, but Cuba was old hat. Since I had been eighteen I had taken a vacation there every year with some of my buddies. Back then you could go to Florida and fly to Cuba for thirty bucks for three or four days. We'd live with native families, gamble, tell each other lies about the native girls—that kind of thing.

On board the *Robinson*, though, life was a little different. I was sort of happy being at sea but it wasn't all it was cracked up to be. You couldn't go "sailing across the bounding main" like they say in the recruiting posters because we were tied up in Guantanamo. The big thing to do every day was go out and learn how to load the antiaircraft guns. I was first loader, and I got a little tired of it after two weeks.

Luckily, though, the Navy had other plans for me. One afternoon I was sitting on board and a courier came alongside with a message. This smart little ensign who didn't much like me called me into his office.

"I don't know how you did it," he said, "but you're going to Norfolk."

I hadn't done anything. Yet here I was being assigned to SACLANT: Supreme Allied Command Atlantic, the eastern hemisphere headquarters of NATO. My job was to produce a five-minute radio show reporting on what NATO was doing. The show went out over about forty stations on Armed Forces Radio as a public service. That was how I ended up doing a program on the cookbook the admiral's wife had put together. I even got the thing promoted on the *Today Show* with my old buddy Frank Blair.

As nice as this little Navy radio job was, however, it wasn't enough to keep me busy. So about a month after I got to Norfolk, I decided to do some freelancing with the local commercial stations.

To get a job, I took a lot of dimes, went into a phone booth, and called every radio station listed in the Yellow Pages. I did this for about a week and a half until finally one of the program directors gave in. "Well, we do need somebody on Sunday," he said.

I didn't give him a minute to change his mind. "You've got him," I said.

That's how I became a disc jockey at WAVY radio. WAVY played a hit list called the *Nifty Fifty*. The big records that year were "Witch Doctor" by David Seville, and "Wake Up Little Susie" by the Everly Brothers.

I called myself Scotty Watty Doo Dah Day, and between my name and the *Nifty Fifty*, my show earned the number one rating in the Tidewater Area in my time slot. Within a year I was the most well-to-do seaman in the Navy. I lived high on the hog wih my own apartment and a '56 T-bird equipped with a sun roof and a convertible top.

Ironically, it was the good life that almost got me in big trouble. One morning I woke up pretty much destroyed from a night out on the town. I dragged myself out of bed, put on my little sailor suit, and went to the office. The guys all wanted some food, so I went back out to the canteen to pick up coffee and Danish for everyone.

As I walked out of the canteen with my hands full of food, a Marine captain was drilling sixty or seventy Marines for some kind of ceremony. I spotted a guy I recognized and kind of waved. All of a sudden, I heard a shout.

"Sailor!"

I wheeled around and said, "Yes sir, Captain."

"What are you supposed to do when you pass an officer?" he barked.

"Salute," I said.

"Salute," he said.

"My hands are full," I answered.

"Damn it, you salute me," he shouted, and he came over and knocked the stuff out of my hands. Of course, I saluted.

He could have put me away for a court-martial for being insubordinate. The thing that saved me was that he chewed me out in front of these sixty jarheads. He cussed me up one side and down the other, telling me that my hat was too small, which it was, and that my uniform was dirty, which it also was.

All the Marines were laughing as he poked me with one of those swagger sticks. It was total humiliation. Finally, he dismissed me.

Two or three days later I found out that he was my next-door neighbor in the apartment complex where I lived off the base. His name was Captain Bill Walker, and we became the best of friends.

I never regretted my Navy days for one minute. One thing I learned from the whole experience is that everything you do has value. The regimentation was good for me, and to this day I believe every kid should be subjected to military duty. There's order there, based on a healthy kind of organization and discipline.

What's more I made some friendships in the Navy that have lasted to this day. In the service there's a camaraderie with other men that you just can't get any-place else and that you can't really explain. It's things like guys sharing latrine duty or getting drunk together, talking dirty, telling jokes and then puking and still liking each other after it's all over. There's just something about it. It has nothing to do with being macho or superior or keeping the girls out of the club-house. It's the Three Musketeers, all for one and one for all, and all that.

But perhaps the greatest thing my two-year stint for Uncle Sam did for me was help me realize what I wanted out of life. When I got out of the Navy in '58, I knew without a doubt that I wanted to come back to NBC. On the surface, at least, it seemed like a safe bet for the future. My staff-announcing job was waiting for me. And so was the *Joy Boys* radio show with Eddie Walker. I knew I had a good thing going at NBC, and I didn't want to rock the boat.

I'm not a gambler at heart. My idea of a good time in those days was to have fifty cents in my pocket and three savings bonds. I don't go out looking for the big risk that's going to earn me a million dollars or the big break that's going to skyrocket me to fame. I'm happy to do my job. I like things the way they are, without pressure, without conflict.

I've always been a little bit like Ferdinand the Bull. One reason I liked him was that he was the gentlest animal in the world and didn't want any kind of conflict. He loved life the way it was and was content to sit under the cork tree and smell the flowers.

Then a bee stung him and he went crazy, snorting and jumping all over the field and leaping fences. Unfortunately for Ferdinand, at that very moment some matadors who were scouting ferocious bulls happened to come by. They were so impressed they rounded him up, put him in a stockade, and got him ready for the bullring. Poor Ferdinand didn't understand what was happening. When he came out, the crowd cheered and yelled because he was big and they thought he would really put up a fight.

But when the senoritas started throwing flowers at the matador, Ferdinand rolled over and started smelling them. The crowd booed in disgust, and Ferdinand was sent home where he belonged.

When I got out of the Navy, I knew where I belonged. I'm an NBC man. If I were Japanese, I'd be out there every morning screaming the company song. The way I had it figured, I'd go back to the company I loved, doing a job I loved, and spend the rest of my days joyfully sniffing the flowers.

I had it figured wrong. What I hadn't counted on was a new boss who came on board not long after I got back from the Navy. From the moment we met I felt he was out to get me. He didn't like me one bit and he threatened to destroy my career at NBC. During the next few years I was pitted against this guy at every turn. Like Ferdinand in the bullring, I was at the center of conflicts and pressures I had sought to avoid.

As problems came up with this guy, it literally took the wisdom of Solomon for me to keep on an even keel at work. King Solomon didn't get his reputation for nothing, I discovered. In the Book of Proverbs he set down two rules of thumb which sum up everything I learned about how to stay happy—and employed.

Rule #1: If you are sensible, you will control your temper. When someone wrongs you, it is a great virtue to ignore it. (Proverbs 19:11 TEV) This tip from Solomon probably saved my career. I had been doing a radio show every morning for about five years when my nemesis, the station's new general manager, was hired. One of his first official acts was to order me to go on at night. The truth was that he wasn't even sure if he wanted me on at all, and by changing my time slot he was really demoting me. But instead of fighting back, I followed Solomon's advice, bit my tongue, and said, "Fine, I'll do it."

But that wasn't enough for my boss. "I want to hear a tape," he said. "I want to hear what you sound like at night."

"Listen to me in the morning," I said.

"I want you to have a different mood at night," he retorted.

I was furious. After five years on the air I was being asked to "audition" for a simple radio show. It was an insult, the straw that *should* have broken the camel's back. But this camel wasn't ready to be broken. I had enough going for me that I could have gotten a job at another station. But I loved NBC so much and felt so much at home that I gave him a tape.

It wasn't exactly the tape he had asked for, however. I took a tape from the show I had done that morning, switched the commercials around, and dubbed in the time as though it were evening. He heard it and said, "Fine."

By going the extra mile, I stayed at NBC. If I had walked out at that point, I probably would have been walking out on my later opportunity with the *Today Show*. Who knows what might have happened? All I know is, by choosing to ignore his insult on that issue and by holding my tongue, I came out ahead.

That approach also saved the *Joy Boys*, which was about to get the ax from this guy. Eddie and I had been doing the show for years, and we knew it was a success, but the manager didn't like it. He didn't understand the humor. The advertisers supported us, but it didn't do any good. The station manager put our show on at the worst possible time. We were given the "ash pit": night-time radio, eight to midnight. We were competing against prime-time television and the summer cookouts. It's an incredible combination to go up against.

But rather than fight and risk losing everything, we took what we could get. We took that show, worked ourselves to the bone for it, and in three years made it the number one show in the District.

We had been wronged, but as Solomon advised, we ignored the wrong and the *Joy Boys* carried on. Even more important to my career, though, was the discovery that I, too, could be wrong.

Rule #2: Hate stirs up trouble, but love forgives all offenses. (Proverbs 10:12 TEV) This may sound namby-pamby, but one thing I learned through all my run-ins with my boss was that the solution to the problem often started with me. I knew he didn't like me, and in response, my attitude toward him just became more negative, out of proportion to the offense. My evil thoughts toward the guy finally became an obsession with me. You know how it is: You start muttering to yourself under your breath.

To me, this man was a monkey on my back. I didn't want to be near him.

At the office, I managed to dodge him as much as I could. But then he invited me to a party he was giving for the whole station. I couldn't really avoid going, since everybody in the office would be there. So I went, hoping I could sneak out at the earliest opportunity.

There, at the party, I met the girl he was going to marry. She was natural, bright, alive, and down to earth. In an instant my attitude toward my boss was transformed. After all, how could a girl like this care for anybody who wasn't all right?

Then a funny thing happened. Once my attitude toward him changed, his changed toward me as well. In fact, it changed so much that during the next few years we became good friends and my career blossomed.

CHAPTER 10

Wedded to Marriage

I became both a husband and a clown within thirty-six hours, but this fact isn't necessarily meant to be a commentary on my marriage. It's just the way things happened.

On August 7, 1959, I married the former Mary Dwyer in her sister Bunkie's house in Washington, D.C. On August 10, I became Bozo the Clown, the host of a new kiddie show on WRC–TV that was to be my proving ground in television.

My marriage, though, was another sort of proving ground. At least the wedding went smoothly enough. The best man was Herman, and the minister who married us was none other than my old college dean, John Bentley, who also happened to be an ordained Methodist preacher. As usual, the crusty Scotsman didn't mince words when he got me alone in a corner before the ceremony and laid down the law.

"Let me tell you something, you bastard," said Bentley. "I've never had one person I've married ever get a divorce. If I'm dead in the grave, I'll come back and haunt you!"

The minute the words left his lips, I took them to heart. Everybody has problems, and over the years Mary and I have had ours. But whenever things looked shaky, I remember thinking, "I can't get a divorce. He'll come back and get me."

The first time that thought crossed my mind was just a few weeks after we were married. Mary and I were sitting on the front stoop of our house feeling kind of blue. I looked at her and she looked at me, and she said what was on both our minds.

"What have we done?" she said.

"I don't know," I said, knowing full well she was referring to our marriage. "I guess we kind of lost our minds. But let's don't panic and do or say something we'd regret. Let's just wait and see what happens."

Mary and I had known each other for only about eight months before we got married. At the time we met, I was engaged to another girl, my heartthrob whom I'd known since I was twelve. I'm not a drifter. I sort of stick to things, and I had stuck with this girl through thick and thin. I was crazy about her, too crazy, actually.

You know how it is when you fall violently in love with somebody. You act like a stupid idiot. You're so head over heels that your life is a combination of tongue-twisters and gaffes, and everything you do seems wrong. You're constantly waiting to correct what you just did.

That *may* be love, but it's certainly not *real*. It's not the kind of love you can live with day in and day out, the kind of love that lets you relax and be yourself. Once I got out of the Navy and reached the point of "Willard maturity," I knew that this girl and I would never make it over the long haul. I guess she knew it too, because she dumped me.

When I met Mary, she was working at WRC and was going with a friend of mine. We all tooled around together, and eventually Mary and I became a twosome.

When it comes to women, I've always known what I wanted, and I knew Mary was what I wanted. She was a hot-tempered Irish girl who was everything I wasn't. She was analytical and had a marvelous mind, not to mention the fact that she was petite and cute as a button. As for me, I've got to admit that I was a darn good catch at the time, too. I was twenty-five, I had thirty or forty thousand dollars in the bank, and I even had hair!

But despite all we had going for us, our marriage didn't exactly get off to a storybook start. We had a heck of a problem the first five or six years. We fought like cats and dogs. We would fight over nothing. It was mainly a clash of personalities.

One time things got to such a state that she hauled off and hit me with a pot. We were in the kitchen talking about something when all of a sudden we got in a screaming match. I can't even remember what we were arguing about. All I can remember is that Mary became violent and shouted, "I hate you, I hate you." Then she grabbed a saucepan and beat me over the chest and dented the thing. I picked up a thermos bottle and threw it at her as she ran down the steps. Thank goodness I missed her. It broke the screen door.

116

Mary may have gotten physical, but I was worse. I was a *mental* bruiser. For example, once I made her cry in a restaurant. We'd been fighting over the fact that she didn't iron my undershirts. "My mother ironed my undershirts," I said, "I don't want a wrinkled under-shirt that comes out of the dryer."

She went into the ladies' room to cry, and there was a woman in there who had heard our whole conversa-tion. The lady told Mary to go back and hit me in the mouth.

What saved our marriage was polyester, polyester "no-iron" undershirts. What really saved us, though, was being willing to give in to each other. After one of these shouting bouts, I'd stonewall it for a few days and say absolutely nothing. Mary would work hard at say-ing nothing, too. But inevitably, one of us would come around and say he was sorry. It never reached the point where both of us stayed stubborn and carried a grudge.

The truth is that I couldn't stay stubborn for long. She had me cornered. At work, if there was a conflict, I could simply stick my nose up, walk away, and ignore it. But with Mary it was different. I slept with her. We were together constantly, and there was no place for me to hide. It was all up front. If there was a problem, I had to face it squarely.

Besides, we were friends, and I couldn't stay mad at a friend for long. We were such good friends that it didn't bother me a bit to have her take off for Europe with a girl friend after we'd been married for about six months. Maybe it should have bothered me, but it didn't. I was just glad for her to have fun. Now, after twenty-two years, I don't like to be away from her even for two days.

There were times in those early years, though, when we both thought about taking a permanent vacation from each other. In the end we stuck it out, but not because of any great strength of character on either of our parts. All along I've felt a divine hand in our marriage. Today I can say with absolute conviction that anything that has been as beautiful as our relationship should never be destroyed. But that feeling came with time.

Over the years, we both began that wonderfully subtle change that takes place when you finally understand that you are "meshing gears," as I call it. The "old you" dies hard. But eventually the two of you do become one. You don't become one when you say "I do." You become one after you've been through the ordeal of fire, the test of strength.

You shave a little of your ego and she shaves a little of hers. You've both been hurt and you've both been exhilarated. In short, you've been through enough of life together to say "This is worth keeping." At that point you've taken on enough of her and she's taken on enough of you that you are truly one in heart, soul, mind, and body.

Enough of Mary's personality and thinking have rubbed off on me, and enough of me has rubbed off on her, that we have grown together. There are certain strengths she's had all along that I've needed. For example, I'm sometimes too passive. I'm the kind who stands in back of a restaurant and waits to be served. Mary is more forceful, but she's never pushy. She's always been dignified and gracious about asserting herself. Over the years I've picked up a little bit of that myself.

Also, when it comes to my work, Mary has always

118

helped keep my ego in line. She worked in broadcasting, and so she knows what TV people are like. She's never been crazy about all the prima donnas and egomaniacs that are in this business, and she's not impressed or swayed by celebrities of any sort. I became a big fish in a little pond in Washington, thanks to Bozo and then the weather job. But she never flaunted it to others. It just wasn't that important to her.

Unfortunately, a lot of spouses of TV people are so totally suppressed that they end up reacting in a strange way to things. Nine times out of ten they're aggressive and more likely to be hard and cynical than gentle and upbeat.

But Mary has always maintained her own life separate from the show-biz world, and that's helped me keep one foot in reality. Early on, we compromised and decided that our social life would not mix with business. As a result, we very rarely hang around with the people I work with.

We also compromised instinctively in our roles around the house. The old male role—the way Herman was—I never could identify with. I was one of the original new breed of husbands. As I look back on it, Mary and I seem to have been about a hundred years ahead of our time. Because my job gave me lots of free time during the day, I was around a lot when our two daughters were growing up. I changed the kids, cleaned the house. To this day I do the dishes almost as much as Mary does. I don't think about it in those terms, though. I don't mind cleaning the floor or doing the bathrooms in our New York apartment or at our home in the country. I never give it a thought.

What really brought us together, though, were two commonplace events—a birth and a death—the kind of thing that every family on earth has confronted since creation. But for us, these events took on a significance that went to the very soul of our marriage.

The first was the birth of our first child, Mary, nearly two years after we were married. It was a sobering moment. There were just me and my wife, but together we had created a human. That little girl was the end result of ten thousand years of Scotts and Phillipses and Woodruffs and Dwyers all the way down the line.

The second watershed was the death of Mary's father. There are only a few times in our lives when we are able to give something to somebody that can make a tremendous difference in their lives. With us, her father's death was an opportunity for me to show her that I loved her—by being her friend, by helping, and by being sympathetic. I loved her father and felt genuinely sorry when he died. But Mary was the one who needed me, and I was able to give her everything I could.

Deep down, all husbands and wives need each other desperately. I know I need Mary. What I need most is a sense of commitment. I need to know that she is 100 percent committed to me and she needs to know that I'm 100 percent committed to her. The night her father died, that sense of togetherness was there for both of us. We realized that after we had invested all these years together, and gone through all this hell, anguish, anxiety, struggling, and fighting, we really were two peas in a pod. And the pod was a mighty nice place to be.

What all this adds up to is that once you've given those marital gears a chance to mesh, the idea of divorce is an affront to your intelligence. It's like a kid who's spent all day at the beach, starting at six o'clock in the morning, working in the sand with his little truck and his little shovel. Finally, at the end of the day, he's built this marvelous sand castle. He has little tunnels that go under it, and he's got little parapets, and he's got little flags stuck into it. Then, in a moment of passion, he comes along and kicks the dickens out of it.

That's exactly what people do to marriage. It's not romantic to put it in those terms. But it's reality. People spend years building up a foundation for a deep, joyful marriage and family life, and then they turn around and throw it all over for some quick thrill.

The TV business is full of stories like the couple who got married early in life when the guy worked in a radio station making 50 bucks a week on the all-night shift. All of a sudden, five years later he's catapulted into a big, high-paying job. The combination of being interviewed by *Time* magazine, having his picture on the back of every in-flight magazine, and seeing his face over national TV goes to his head. He can't stand the fact that his first wife remembers when he was nothing and was making nothing. She can't resist reminding him of it and he can't resist getting rid of her when another one comes along who says she adores him.

Now, I'm not saying it can't be beautiful to remarry if the first one was lousy. Many people find far more happiness the second time around. But the sad thing is the way people treat this whole marriage relationship from the start. They don't really think it's for keeps.

The way I see it, half the people who end up in divorce got married to begin with because they were caught up in a physical attraction. At some point in their life, sex has dominated and ruled. But that's not all there is to marriage. It's a great part of it—we all know that—but that's not *it*.

"It" is something much, much deeper. Let's say you

married at twenty-five and now you're fifty. One day, you roll over in bed and take a good look at this person next to you. She has given you children. She's not only your wife, your partner in sex, and the lady that takes care of your socks; she's also what's left of your family. Over the years, your mother has died, and your father has died. Those kids in the next room are going away to school or they'll be getting married. So, here you are, just the two of you. The two of you together are *it*. She is your family—your life, your history, and your roots. And you're hers.

The way I see it, divorce is symptomatic of the self-centered, egotistical, self-serving, pleasure-seeking, short-term world we live in. These days it's almost a status symbol to have two or three husbands or wives. Some experts are even telling us that longevity being what it is, we should actually *plan* on having a second marriage, just like we might plan for a second career or a second house.

It's also becoming more of a status symbol to cheat on your husband or wife. One recent poll showed that more than half the wives in the country have had an affair. Twenty-five years ago affairs took a lot more work. Today, you get in a car, go to the drugstore, and go to a motel. And that's it.

You can't be married and do that. If you want to go out and sleep with everything that walks, don't get married! But also, don't try to pretend you have a family because a family must have love and trust and commitment. And commitment begins with faithfulness to each other.

I don't care how you slice it: You can put it any way you want to. You get married and the flesh becomes one. You become one person. You are that person's mate. You can tell me how great it is to swing, or about the pleasures of group sex and hot tubs until it comes out of your ear. But I don't believe there's any way that kind of lifestyle is going to work. You can't be married and fool around.

For one thing, you can't really conceal these things for long. That's where people lie to themselves. They have really overlooked the laws that govern these things. But there are certain absolutes you can't ignore. They're there, and they mean something. A couple of times when I was young and single, I remember going to bars, getting drunk, and doing things I shouldn't have. I also remember the total emptiness the next day, the feeling that it was dirty, sleazy, and cheap.

That feeling is the exact opposite of the joy you can experience in a marriage. By ignoring those absolutes, you're going to pay a tremendous price. Keep it up and you're going to lose everything. You're going to lose that fabulous deep love that arises from an unwavering commitment to another human being. You're going to lose the feeling of total acceptance you get from a spouse who's been with you through everything. You're going to lose those golden moments together on Christmas Eve.

In short, you're going to end up in a midlife crisis when you could be going through a midlife revival in your marriage. A good marriage is like an incredible retirement fund. You put everything you have in it during the best years of your productive life, and over the years it has turned from silver to gold to platinum. I mean, it has become the rarest gem.

Most people want to be part of the kind of love I'm talking about. But too many don't want to sign their names on the dotted line. They're afraid of absolutes.

123

If there were only some way we could bottle absolutes and label them and sell them like we do soap and underarm deodorants, we'd be doing a land-office business in happiness. You could have a commercial every day for "Thou shalt not covet thy neighbor's wife." We could do it like they do *Sesame Street*—things popping out of the screen every few minutes. People would be falling all over themselves to get an absolute or two, because everybody has some kind of conscience.

Fortunately for me, guilt has helped hold my life together, especially when it comes to marriage, and I don't think that's a bad thing at all. I believe in rewards. I believe in punishments. I believe in sin and right and wrong and conscience, and I respond to that kind of thing.

It's a lucky thing, too. Because three days after I was married, my commitment to Mary was put to the test when WRC–TV sent me to Hollywood, the city that put guilt on the map. That's where I was supposed to learn the tricks and gimmicks of Bozo the Clown.

CHAPTER 11

Clowning Around with Kids

There's really no secret to working with kids. It all comes down to two things, loving them, and letting them know it. They can sense your feelings almost like little animals. If you communicate love or feelings of warmth, they'll respond.

I always liked kids, even before I had my own. When I was in high school I volunteered to teach Vacation Bible School every summer, just because I got a kick out of being with kids.

It was only natural, I guess, for me to take instantly to working with kids as a professional clown, first as Bozo, the TV clown whom kids adored, and then as America's number one clown, Ronald McDonald, a character I created in Washington.

My first chance to do kiddie shows professionally actually came before I was in the Navy, on a Saturday TV show called *Barn Party*. I was "Farmer Willard," and I played opposite a very refined lady named Betsy Stelk, who had a fairyland aura about her. To round out the show, we had an innovative bunch of puppets created by a guy named Jim Henson. They were called the Muppets, and *Barn Party* was one of their first shows on television. I worked with a bald-headed Muppet with a big nose, named Sam, sort of the way Fran Allison worked on *Kukla, Fran and Ollie*. Then there was the frog named Kermit. I used to do a commercial with him for a local peanut butter called Schindlers. He'd open his mouth, I'd give him a big spoonful, and he'd go "ahh." Kermit was the only Muppet to survive *Barn Party*.

When Bozo came along, I was in the big time of children's television, and I was getting paid to do what I always loved to do. Bozo was a syndicated clown show started by a guy named Larry Harmon. WRC had bought the rights to do the TV show in Washington. I got into the act because I was a staff announcer, and staff announcers did everything. It was cheaper for the station to use a staff announcer for something like this because if they got a freelancer they'd have to pay twice as much. At the time, I was about twenty-five, just out of the Navy, and all the other staff announcers were at least fifteen to twenty years older than I was. They had either had heart attacks or hernia operations and none of them was fit to do the clown show.

That's why three days after I got married I found myself on a plane heading for "clown school" at the Bozo the Clown studios in Hollywood. The minute I touched down in California it was show-biz all the way.

I was met at the airport by some public relations people from the Bozo show who had tear sheets from *Variety* to impress me that my name was in print. Then I was wined and dined in typical Hollywood fashion.

It was everything you've ever imagined about Hollywood. At one party I rubbed shoulders with an elderly movie mogul who was there with a girl who looked young enough to be his granddaughter. The PR guy had this book filled with girls' names and he offered to set me up with a hot little number to keep me company during my stay. The fact that I was just married didn't mean a thing to him. I thanked him politely and preserved my "honor."

Another night the PR guy took me to dinner at his home in Coldwater Canyon, about two hills away from Frank Sinatra's house. His wife had been Cecil B. De-Mille's secretary. She had on a blue chiffon lounging gown and held a little poodle in her arm. Mama had a little blue bow in her hair, and the poodle had a little blue bow in his.

The host showed me around the house and took me to see the bathroom that had been specially built for his wife. The tub was all glass enclosed and it sort of hugged the hill overlooking Los Angeles. It had gold fixtures with swans, and water seemed to shoot out of the wall.

As the sun set over Santa Monica, you could look out over LA as it was getting dark and see the lights, which seemed to sparkle like diamonds. I guess that's why the host had dubbed the bathroom "baby's jewel box."

That's the way it went for the two weeks I spent at clown school. Actually, the school was nothing more than a set where I would learn how to talk and act like Bozo. The Bozo set was right next to the one where they shot *Gunsmoke*. One of the most exciting things was seeing James Arness—all seven feet of him—strut across the studio lot. The next most exciting thing was seeing Charlie Weaver drive up in a Plymouth convertible that was filled to overflowing with beautiful starlets. I was impressed.

But most impressive of all was Bozo's creator, Larry Harmon. He picked me up in his huge red Cadillac with leopardskin upholstery and took me to lunch at the Brown Derby. The car had a speaker with a microphone, and every time he saw a kid on the street he would go into his clown routine: "This is Bozo—huh, huh, huh."

Harmon was an actor, writer, and producer who had done Bozo's voice for the "talking books" Capitol Records had made famous in the forties. Back then, the big record companies were Victor and Decca. Capitol was just a fledgling company that a lot of top singers had put some money into. The company wasn't making any money until Bozo came along.

Through Capitol's "talking books," a kid could learn to read by listening to the story of Bozo on a 78 record and following along in a book that came with it. At the end of each page, a little bell would go off that told the kid it was time to turn to the next one.

Bozo and the "talking books" made enough money to put Capitol over the top. About ten years later, in the mid-fifties Harmon got enough money to buy the record rights to Bozo from Capitol and start a children's show for television, featuring a live Bozo character whose costume, make-up, voice, and gestures he invented. He got an animator and put together about 150 Bozo the Clown cartoons. Then he syndicated the show and sold it to 183 local TV stations. WRC in Washington was one of the first stations to sign on.

The format of the show was pretty standard. Ours was an hour long, with a peanut gallery. The show opened with cartoons, and then I was supposed to swing out across the studio on a rope which was about three feet off the ground, yelling, "Hi boys and girls." I got the routine down pat at clown school, where I learned how to fall, and how to do the Bozo voice.

I wore a typical baggy clown suit with a red wig, oversized clown shoes, and a bulbous nose. Once our show got underway on WRC, I added my own touches to the Bozo character. One Willard touch was a "squeaky nose." The squeak came from a horn I had pinned to my undershirt underneath my costume. When the kids in the peanut gallery came around, I'd ask their names and tweak their noses with my fingers. As I was tweaking, I'd hit the horn with my left arm. Then the kids would tweak my nose and the horn would go off again.

Another thing I added was something I called "Bozo Ball." I was always big on audience participation, and so I got the kids at home involved in the show by throwing a colorful beach ball directly to the camera. I had the kids at home write in their name and their school, and then I'd say, "Okay, Tom, we have the ball coming right to you." The ball would go right into the camera and the kids at home would go crazy.

But it turned out that there was much more to doing Bozo than just throwing balls and tweaking noses. For me, the role was a tremendous training ground for a television career.

Right from the start I learned to lose all inhibitions in front of the camera. When you're playing to kids, you don't have time to be self-conscious. The important thing is to put on a good show for the peanut gallery, and the result is that you become so engrossed in performing that you become natural and let loose with everything you've got.

I learned what it meant to put on a good show during the taping of the first pilot for the program. The girl who did the booking for guests had called a local orphanage to get a busload of kids to appear as the peanut gallery.

The morning of the taping, we were all set to get started when a bus pulled up and all these seventy-year-olds stepped out looking for a good time. What the booking agent didn't realize was that there were two institutions for orphans in Washington. One was called "Junior Village," for orphaned kids, and the other was D.C. village, for old folks who were alone in the world. She had called D. C. village by mistake.

Since this was show-biz, and the show must go on, we put them in the peanut gallery and went on with the Bozo show. I did the show exactly as I would have if they had been a bunch of six-year-olds. First I squeaked their noses and had them squeak mine. After that, I asked their names, and had them play "Bozo ball."

At the end, we gave them some Twinkies and ice cream we had for the kids, and they all had a heck of a time. The ones who are still living still talk about it.

When you work in television, you have to be ready for anything. It's even more true when you're working with kids. They used to pee on me all the time or break wind. There was always a great passing of gas on the show. The little kids used to cut loose because they were so excited.

There were times on the show when all I could do was roll with the punches, literally. Although I could handle most of the kids that came on the show, every once in a while we had a child who had an emotional problem and got so fired up with excitement that he was uncontrollable. I could usually out-talk him or out-wit him. But one morning I met my match.

There were maybe ten to fifteen kids sitting around me in a circle, and out of the corner of my eye I could see this one kid going nutty. His eyes started to flash, his legs were twitching, and he was grinning a lot. I thought maybe he was just excited or wet. But I figured out too late that he was more than just excited. By the time I got to him to tweak his nose, he went bananas.

"Ha, Bozo," he yelled, like some sort of wild Japanese samurai on the attack. Before I knew it, he had pushed me on the floor and was sitting on my stomach beating me up. He was about ten—a Cub Scout in uniform no less—and he was punching my nose and pounding at my face with his hands.

I caught a glimpse of the floor manager offstage, but he was doing absolutely nothing to help. All he had to do was run on the set and pull the kid off me, which he finally did when it came time for the cartoon. The guy claimed he didn't want to go on camera because there was a union rule against it.

For every knock in the head I got as Bozo, though, there were some precious moments that made all the craziness worthwhile. One time, a lady wrote to me to say that her daughter had leukemia and had only a month or two to live. The little girl's favorite TV personality was Bozo, and her mother wondered if I could come over to visit the child in the hospital.

The girl was six or seven, and when I walked into the hospital room I was shocked to see this tiny wizened form. She was white, ghastly white, with barely a breath of life in her frail body. But the minute she saw Bozo, her eyes sparkled and she smiled. For a few minutes, we squeaked noses, and then she gave me a hug goodbye. About four hours later she died.

It was my love for kids, like this little girl, that kept me going during my hectic years as Bozo. It had to be love—or insanity—because the pace I was keeping was exhausting. Along with doing the Bozo show, I worked a regular eight-hour shift as a staff announcer. During the day, I had my radio shows, my TV and radio announcing chores, and the Bozo show every day at five o'clock. At night, I worked as a disc jockey. Most nights I'd sign off the station at 2:00 A.M.

On top of that, on weekends I was off and running making special appearances as Bozo. Saturday and Sunday I'd do Bar Mitzvahs and flea markets—you name it. I think I opened every shopping center in the Washington area.

When a new fast-food hamburger franchise asked me to help open their first store in Alexandria, Virginia, I was only too happy to oblige. The store was called McDonald's, and the local Washington franchise was owned by two brothers who had bought the right to use the famous golden arches and sell hamburgers under the McDonald's name.

At the time, Bozo was the hottest children's show on the air. You probably could have sent Pluto the Dog or Dumbo the Elephant over and it would have been equally as successful. But I was there, and I was Bozo.

After that first opening, I did some commercials for McDonald's, and the whole thing was a big hit. From then on, I made an appearance every time a local McDonald's opened. There were eventually about thirty-five or forty stores all over the Washington area. I remember one opening where five thousand people showed up.

There was something about the combination of hamburgers and Bozo that was irresistible to kids. That's why when Bozo went off the air a few years later, the local McDonald's people asked me to come up with a new character to take Bozo's place.

So, I sat down and created Ronald McDonald. Over the years, lots of people have taken credit for inventing Ronald. But Ronald was really born out of the Bozo show in Washington, and I gave birth to him. I went to a lady named Mrs. Hubbard at Jack Mullane's costume shop in Washington, and told her what I wanted, and she made the original Ronald McDonald costume. The way I conceived him, he was a happy clown, and anything kids liked to do, Ronald did. He swam, he fished, he went on picnics, and he roller-skated.

As Ronald McDonald, I did all the local McDonald's commercials, and soon Ronald became hotter than any kids' show. In fact, he became so hot that for one summer he had his own TV show. I was eating the whole thing up, not to mention enjoying the extra forty grand a year it earned me on top of my salary at WRC.

Just as Ronald was growing in Washington, so was the popularity of McDonald's across the country. The parent company realized they were onto something much bigger with this fast-food business, and they began buying back the franchises in order to have total control over quality. When they got around to Washington, they saw the success of Ronald McDonald and took over the character along with the local franchises.

Everybody made out on that deal except me. I didn't realize what the character was worth, so I had never bothered to copyright it. I'm not even sure I could have. At any rate, I put faith in promises. "You'll be the national Ronald McDonald," I was told. But once the parent company got hold of Ronald, they never gave me so much as a howdy-do. So that's how Ronald and I parted company.

Bozo and I had parted a few years earlier, when the show finally peaked in popularity and came to a natural end. But as much fun as it had been, I can't say I was sorry to see him go. About a month before the show was set to go off the air, I was so tired of it I was almost delirious.

One day, I went in to put on my makeup and my hand started to shake. It scared me, because I thought I was having a nervous breakdown. I had to talk myself into going upstairs, going on the set, and getting on that swing to open the show with a jolly "Hi, boys and girls." Somehow, I made it through that day and to the end of Bozo's run.

But no matter how sick I was of playing Bozo, I never got sick of the kids. To me, they were an endless source of fun, an unpredictable element that added a little punch to life. What I always loved about kids was their sense of wonder. They're born with a joy for life and all it has to offer. To a kid, everything is an exciting event, whether it's a helicopter flying overhead or a Bozo ball coming to the camera. That excitement and joy were infectious and it made me feel good, too.

That's why, when Bozo went off the air, I was only too happy to graduate to a relatively low-key role as "Uncle Willard" hosting reruns of the *Mickey Mouse Show*. I wore mouse ears and a blazer, and my job was to simply open and close the show and do commercials.

What I remember most about that show was the happiness the Mickey Mouse ears brought to one little boy who had come to the studio for a much more serious event. Every Wednesday night a group of Jewish kids came to the studio to tape a show that aired on Sunday, sponsored by the Washington Board of Rabbis. One night, some Orthodox Jewish kids came on. They all had their *yarmulkes* except one little boy who had obviously left his at home. The director wanted to use him on the show, and his parents were upset that he didn't have a *yarmulke*.

So Uncle Willard stepped in. "Wait a minute," I said. "If you folks don't think it's an insult, I think I have the answer to your problem."

I went into the Mickey Mouse office and got some Mickey Mouse ears. We took the ears off and turned the Walt Disney insignia around to the back. The kid was overjoyed as he went on television with what may be the first *yarmulke* ever made from a Mousketeer hat.

There's nothing I do that gives me as much pleasure as bringing joy to a chld. Maybe it's because kids give so much love in return. It was true of the kids in the peanut gallery on TV, and it was even more true of my own children, Mary and Sally.

If you want to experience love in its purest form, the place to start is with your very own kids. If there's such a thing as pure, uncut love that's 100 percent, the best stuff in the world, guaranteed foolproof, it's the love a parent can have for his child.

But a lot of people these days think that life is more fun without kids. I guess I can't look down my nose at that. I've known good people who knew what they wanted out of life, and what they wanted didn't include kids. They preferred to live alone, just the two of them, with a nice little TR–3, and maybe a little cat and a lot of travel.

That's okay. But I think it's sad to deprive yourself of

the incredible affection you can experience with a child. It's not the same in any way as love of a spouse. But I honestly believe it's the most powerful love in the whole world.

There are even some parents who deny that love, and cut themselves off from the tremendous potential for joy that's right there for the asking. When I played Bozo, it was a total shock for me to discover that there are parents who simply do not like their kids. I could tell it by the way they acted when they brought their kids to the peanut gallery. Those parents didn't have to say a word to communicate the fact that they were bored to death and had no interest in anything the kid was interested in. They looked like they were just tolerating the whole thing.

It was a baffling attitude to me, coming from the kind of home I did, where my mother would put me first in everything, and where my father always paticipated in the things I did.

How many of those kids ended up thumbing their noses at their parents later on, I can only guess. I've seen parents who get nothing but total rebellion from their children. Anything they tell the kids, the kids will sass back.

I've often wondered, are these kids rebellious by nature? I don't think so. I think a lot of kids turn sour because they feel like they're not important to their parents. They see their parents so involved in so many other things that they feel insignificant. They think they're not worth much, and if they've done anything at all, they've messed up their parents' lives. In other words, if they weren't around, their parents would be much better off.

On the other hand, if you're a kid, and you feel like

your parent needs you, then you have an automatic importance in this world and you feel confident within your self.

There's no secret to being a good parent, just as there's no secret to working with kids on TV. Again, all you have to do is love them and let them know it. As a parent, you set the tone for the relationship with your children from the day they're born. It's all in the attitude you communicate.

You can communicate that you enjoy being with them, or you can give them the signals that you really have other things to do that are more important. You can let them know that you accept them totally and unconditionally, or you can expect them to measure up to some standard of perfection that none of us can ever achieve. And you can communicate that you need them just as much as they need you, or you can imply that your life would be better without them.

My daughters know I'd break an appointment with anybody in the world to be with them. That's how much I love their company. I was blessed and very fortunate because I could be around them a lot as they were growing up. I changed them and washed their little butts, burped them and fetched their formula, certainly as much as Mary did. If Mary had a meeting or wanted to shop downtown, I was always there to babysit as long as she got home by five so I could go to work.

I never resented it one bit. Having that constant relationship with my daughters brought me a joy and pleasure most fathers miss. Today many more men seem to like the idea of changing diapers or going to the park with the kids. To me this is one really good sign I see in the new generation.

A lot of people miss out on life by putting up a sophisticated front. There's a well of life you can drink deeply from by experiencing things close at hand. How many people skim the surface on everything, including love and personal relationships? That's especially true of a relationship with a child. Once it's gone, it's gone. You can never recapture those moments.

As for discipline, I've never hit those kids in my life. The only time I ever came close to it was one time when Little Mary was beating one of our dogs with a stick while I was talking on the telephone. I threw the phone book at her. It missed, but she got the message.

I've always gotten out of them what I needed to without spanking, even to this day. I never have to say "Sally, go do your homework," or "Mary, go feed the dog right now." Fortunately, it's never been like that. It's almost matter-of-fact with us that we all pitch in and help without being asked.

What it comes down to, I think, is that they really want to please me because they know I want to please them. I get the biggest kick out of doing things for them and doing things with them. When the girls were growing up, Mary and I never took a vacation without them. We never even considered it.

I don't want my kids to do anything for me out of fear. I'm not interested in authority. I'm interested in their love. I want that to motivate them. If I have to beat somebody to get obedience, I don't want that kind of respect. I don't want it with friends, with my wife, or with anybody.

I have to admit, though, that my kids have had it kind of easy when it comes to pressures to perform. Unlike a lot of parents, I've never been demanding about schoolwork or money because I don't care much for either myself. I'm not saying my approach is good or bad; it's just the way I am.

I told them to get the heck out of school as fast as they could without cheating. If they came home with a D in something, I'd say, "Good for you, you didn't flunk it." If they flunked it, I'd say, "Take it again." If they had trouble with math, my attitude was "Get rid of it as quickly as possible."

Education is overrated (here's my hillbilly Southern red-neck coming out!). The way I see it, there's been more time wasted in the past twenty-five years by some kids who went to college who had no business being there. Dean Bentley said that once in class, and I agreed with him. He looked out and half of us were asleep, and he said, "You know something. Half of you shouldn't even be here." He was right. We shouldn't have been there. I was only there to get the diploma. The fact that I went to college hasn't made one single difference in my life, except for my meeting Eddie Walker. In terms of dollars and cents, though, I wouldn't have made one nickel more.

When it comes to money, my girls have never gotten an allowance. If there's money in my wallet and they want it, it's theirs. None of us has ever been too good about appreciating money. I guess it's just in the genes.

But even if we may not have a lot of rules in our house, we do have a lot of communication. I look for practical things to tell them, like "Don't drink whiskey because it rots your brain," or "Don't smoke because it gives you emphysema," or "Don't sleep around because old habits are tough to break." I tell them you can't have it both ways if you want an unpolluted well of love and happiness in your marriage. You can't pee in the well just a little and expect it not to make any difference. You'll still have dirtied the water.

Whether it's sex or drugs or whatever, I've never said "Don't you dare do this or that." I tell each one simply that if she can't handle it and if something happens, there's nobody in the world that can help her. There's nothing I can do. I'll stand by her, certainly. But no amount of money or moral support will buy back your soul once it's been lost.

I don't pretend that they've always followed my advice to the letter. But at least they know where I stand.

In the end, all you can really do for your kids is guide them. There are some bad seeds, and there are some who just have a screw loose somewhere. But I believe if you love a kid enough—and only you know whether you do—they'll turn out all right in the end.

For me, though, the payoffs have been there all along, in the love and respect my daughters have shown me. I've also been paid back a hundredfold by the kids who watched me on television.

All those years of squeaking noses, playing Bozo ball, and appearing as Ronald McDonald brought me the joyful affection of a generation of kids in the Washington area. I found that out when I became WRC's weatherman. By then, those kids had moved on to college or to jobs. They were tuning into the news every night, and they still were my most loyal fans.

CHAPTER 12

Even a Gorilla Could Be a Weatherman

There's an old story that's made the rounds at the National Weather Service about the Indian who predicted the weather. He was a sanctimonious old guy with a blanket wrapped around him and long pigtails. Because Indians are supposed to have an uncanny ability to predict the weather, every morning the guys at the Weather Service would consult him.

They'd ask him what the weather was and he'd say, "Cloudy," or "Rainy."

One morning this guy gets up and says to the Indian, "What's the weather going to be?"

"Don't know," says the Indian.

"Why not?" asks the guy.

"Radio broke," says the Indian.

It's a corny story but it says everything there is to say about what it takes to be a weatherman on television. All you really need is the right image and the right person to call at the National Weather Service.

A trained gorilla could do it. When I was pegged as WRC's weatherman in the late sixties, I had the right image. What with Vietnam, race riots, and college protests, by the time the weather came on at 11:15 P.M., people were ready for a little clowning around.

I guess the station figured that after ten years as Bozo and Ronald McDonald, I could bring a little joy into viewer's lives. I gave them everything I could. I was an event waiting to happen. I was chomping at the bit waiting to go wild. And as the weatherman, I was given free rein to be as wild as I wanted.

On Groundhog Day I dressed up like a groundhog and was filmed at the Washington Monument emerging from a manhole. TV viewers got a shot of my furry hand reaching out of the hole. Then they saw this 260-pound groundhog race down the mall past the White House.

Another time, for Mother's Day, I dressed up like a woman with a wig and cleavage, and I pulled the forecast out of my bosom. I wore a barrel once on Income Tax Day. It was an old whiskey barrel, and I looked like I was naked except for the barrel—really far-out stuff.

I played it as cornball as I ever did. Everyone in town knew me from the clown days so I could get away with it. I even brought animals on the show, like the 800-pound black bear named Gentle Ben who did a walk-on. I said, "Will you hand me the forecast for tomorrow?" Then the bear walked on and gave me a piece of paper. I gave him a kiss in return. Do you know how you kiss bears? The secret I learned from circus people is to put a piece of green pepper in your lips and say,

"Give me a kiss." Bears love green pepper, and what the bear really does is take the pepper out of your lips.

Stunts like this made the audience go wild. The crazier it was the more the viewers loved it. But what really drew in the viewers was a gimmick that came about by accident. A school in Bethesda, Maryland, sent me a pink carnation and said, "Would you please announce our school carnival?"

I stuck the flower in my buttonhole and plugged the carnival, opening the door to a flood of viewer mail requesting support for local events. There were tutus and tights from the Opera Society which I wore on the air, broadbrimmed hats with pink birds from garden clubs, and a live bullfrog from the Fairfax County fair.

All of this gave me tremendous viewer identification. The costumes, the flower in my lapel—not to mention the toupee that I took on and off—instantly set me apart from the other weathermen in town.

I didn't think of it in the beginning, but the fact is there's tremendous recall in a flower. If you watch fifteen different weather guys in their polyester suits and they all have cropped hair and glasses but only one has a flower, you're going to remember him. There's a softness about a flower—it represents sensitivity and a certain flair. It conjures up images of all those old movies with Adolphe Menjou and Maurice Chevalier, and the warm, free-spirited style that went with them. In my case, it certainly didn't represent culture. Whatever it represented, it worked.

Not everyone in Washington was enchanted by my act, however. Once I was pushing a shopping cart in a Virginia supermarket when a little old lady charged by and smacked me with her umbrella.

"I can't stand you," she said.

Believe it or not, it was sentiments like that, that made me a success as a weatherman. Television is a funny business. It may be the only profession in the world where negative reactions can actually work in your favor. The stronger your personality on the air, the more people you offend. Recognition is what counts more than anything else when ratings are being tallied. So whether people liked me or hated me, at least they *watched* and *remembered* me.

Another thing I had going for me was that like the old Indian with his radio, I knew where to go for the weather. Ninety-nine percent of the weather comes from the same source, the National Weather Service. After that, there are only so many ways you can say "Partly sunny, chance of showers." You can say "Frontal systems in the Northeast Corridor are causing steering currents aloft and an occluded front across the Mississippi Valley." Or you can say "Tomorrow's going to be partly sunny with a chance of showers." Anybody who can read can do the weather. It's a reporting job. It's not a job in which you go up on the top of a mountain to check winds and make your weather forecast.

I had done the weather for years on radio, as part of my staff announcing duties. I had a two-and-a-half-minute weather show. Originally, the weather report was written for me, but later on I put it together myself. There's nothing to it. You rip it off the wire which feeds you sixteen lines of typed copy in a minute. Then you pick the top stories and underline this or that, and call up the Weather Service and ask them the right questions.

The only difference with television was that now I had to put these magnetic "stickums" that said "cold front" on a map. Before the show, I'd write the temper-

atures in on the map. People always think the weatherman has such a great memory. The truth is you don't
memorize a thing. You take a red pencil and write on
the map, and since the camera doesn't pick up red,
you've got the information right in front of you!

From the very beginning, I had fun doing the weather. I played it loose and casual, because to me it was just
one more job to do. It was a last-minute decision to
make me the weatherman in the first place. The regular
weatherman, a guy who had done the show for twelve
years, decided he didn't want to work at night anymore. He quit on a Friday. The next Monday at 11:00
P.M., I went upstairs to the studio and walked on the set
as the weatherman.

I owe my weather career to a man named Joe Good-
fellow, who was manager of radio and television for
WRC at the time the weather spot opened up. Ironically, he had never been one of my biggest fans.

But for some reason, Joe wouldn't hear of anybody
else but me doing the weather. Several people tried to
talk him out of it. They didn't think I had the back-
ground, the composure, or the right vibrations. They
wanted someone more serious and sober, more of an
authority. But Joe said, "Willard is my weatherman, and
that's final."

I set the record straight at the start. "You all know
more about the weather than I do," I told the viewers.
"I do have the sense to come out of the rain."

Little by little, I became a weatherman. For about a
year I was considered the "audition host" while the station looked for a permanent weatherman. But at some
point the ratings started going up, and before long we
were rated right up there with our big competition,
Louis Allen, who had been on TV for twenty-five years.

Finally, WRC stopped holding auditions for other weathermen, and I knew I had the job.

There's nothing magic in my approach to the weather. I like to joke that I'm not a meteorologist, I'm a professional "mediocratist." I start with the premise that basically people want to know "Is it going to rain tomorrow?" That question is so important that something like 30 to 50 percent of the people who watch the evening news tune in for the weather report and nothing else.

Once you give people the basics, the next most important thing is to know your territory. In Washington, that meant giving a word or two to satisfy the tremendous agricultural interests in the area. Within a hundred-mile range you have farming up in the Pennsylvania Dutch country, in Virginia, and in parts of Maryland, along with orchards and cattle. Then there's what I consider the most beautiful body of water in the United States, Chesapeake Bay. I would always try to include the sea conditions at the Bay all year round, along with wind conditions and ice conditions in the winter.

To me, the weather wasn't just a lot of abstract facts, it was information that affected people. I let those people know that I knew they were out there. In the summer, for example, instead of saying "Hey, another beautiful day," I'd single out a few people who had a stake in the weather that day. For vacationers, I'd say, "It's going to be another sunny day and if you're going on a picnic you'll have fun." For ranchers I'd say, "If you have cattle, you know the water shortage is here."

When it comes to forecasting, I'm no more right or wrong than any other weatherman around because we're all operating from basically the same information. I started doing the weather about the time that computers and weather satellites were first being used. Since then, there's been about an 8 to 10 percent improvement in weather forecasting.

The experts thought that satellites would make a fabulous improvement in forecasting, but they really haven't. Nobody knows why weather systems change. For example, suppose there's a storm in Chicago that's moving southeast. The currents aloft are moving it right along and there's rain in the front and more moisture being fed into it from the Gulf of Mexico. All of a sudden, it goes over the Ohio Valley and rains like a son of a gun. Nobody knows why.

The only accurate forecast is twenty-four hours, and even that's only about 85 percent accurate. After that, it's guesswork or instinct.

There are some weathermen who claim to be able to do long-range forecasting. But as of this writing, *nobody* can do it.

As for almanacs, they base their predictions on cycles. They will go back twelve years to determine what phase of the moon the earth was in, then they will say that 1984 is going to be like the year 1972. They tell you the first day of spring and fall, when the sun rises and sets each day, the phases of the moon, and eclipses. If you believe in astrology, which I don't, they give you all the astrological signs to plant by.

There isn't just one almanac—there are several of them. *The Old Farmer's Almanac*, in Dublin, New Hampshire, is 191 years old and is said to be the oldest continuous publication in America.

The one I like best is the one my grandfather used. It's *J. Gruber's Hagerstown Almanac*, from Hagerstown, Maryland. I pull it out whenever viewers call to ask

147

what the weather will be like two months from now when their daughter's going to get married. I read them what the almanac has to say and tell them, "That's fifty-fifty. You can flip a coin or make up the weather that day and you'll be just as accurate. The odds aren't too bad."

Weather forecasting isn't an exact science, and that's what makes it fun, for me, anyway. Rather than rely on the guesswork of computers and charts of weather cycles, I'd much rather put my money on the signs of nature, and the good old-fashioned instinct of people who can feel the weather in their bones. That old Indian in my story may have used a radio, but a lot of farmers and mariners who live close to the elements know something about the weather we TV weathermen will probably never know.

There are some old Bay people up at the Chesapeake who can smell a change of weather with their noses. The Bay is incredibly unpredictable. Out in the middle of the Bay it can be a beautiful, sunny day, clear, without a cloud in the sky, and in five minutes you can get 75-mile-an-hour winds just like a miniature tornado. They call them "water spouts" and these old mariners can sense them just like the dogs in China that start barking when an earthquake is coming. The mariners can look at the way the water is acting and they can just tell. And they high-tail it out of the center of the Bay as fast as they can.

Some of the old farmers down in Virginia used to follow signs of nature, like watching the dogwood, to decide when to plant corn. They never planted until the dogwood blossoms turned brown. It was common sense, really. After the frost nips them, the dogwood blossoms continue on the tree for a while. When they finally get brown and fall off the tree, it means there aren't going to be any more killing frosts that year. The dogwood comes out in early spring. By the time the petals have fallen, you can be sure there are no more hard frosts because summer is just around the corner!

I get such a kick out of these natural predictors that I've used some of them on the air. I've also gotten pretty good at watching for natural signs myself. One I've never known to fail is spiders. They'll start coming into your house, particularly around doorjambs and windowsills, in the fall. Twenty-four hours after they congregate there's a dramatic change in the weather. Many's the time I'll look and see tremendous movement of spiders in our house, and within twelve to twenty-four hours, the weather will drop from 70 degrees to 40.

Another one I like is the persimmon seeds, which are said to give an indicator of the severity of the cold. You dry out the persimmon, take a knife, and slice a seed down the middle. Inside, there's a little white mole-like growth which will be in the shape of a knife, fork, or spoon. A knife means a severe winter, a fork is a mild one, and a spoon is somewhere in between.

To me, this is the kind of thing that makes the weather so fascinating. It's a never-ending source of interest, and I've turned it into kind of a hobby. At home on my farm in Virginia I have my own weather station. It's a professional setup, not the kind of thing you can pick up for a few bucks at a hardware store. When I'm home, I'll check the anemometer for the wind direction, look at the electronic thermometer for the temperature, and check the barometer and sky conditions.

Over the years I've managed to pick up basic meteorological skills the same way I've picked up farming skills—by simply *doing*. Take my orchard, for example. When I planted my orchard twenty years ago, I didn't know anything about pruning trees. I didn't know how to cut the branches, or that the peach trees are supposed to be wide open in the middle so the sun can get through, or that you have to prune half the peaches that form in May so that the others can get enough sustenance. I didn't know what they thrived on or the best time to fertilize. But things like that, I learned. Now I have one hundred fruit trees and they're all absolutely perfect.

When it comes to the weather, I've had people express doubt that I knew what I was talking about. To a certain extent, they're right. I used to say "It's your money, your government, I'm just giving you their weather forecast."

But beauty in a weatherman is in the eye of the beholder. If you want to think I'm a complete idiot and a buffoon and a jerk and a hillbilly and a bore, I can't change that. That's just me. If you happen to like me, then you'll think I'm a dynamite weatherman and say "Old Willard says."

It's a personality thing. People watch the weatherman they like. It's the same way with doctors. I prefer a doctor who says "There's nothing wrong with your darn knee, just keep from drinking too much, lose some weight, and I don't want to see you again for six months." Other people go for the doctor who tells them "You've got a little arthritis in your knee, take some aspirin once in a while." Still others like a doctor who explains things even more. You "pays your money" and "takes your choice."

On television, though, when people love you, they *really* love you. During my fifteen years doing the weather in Washington, the love and affection I was shown were tremendous. There were those, like the lady with the umbrella, who would have liked to smash me over the head, and others who hated me because I was a fat slob. But most people have shown nothing but love.

Television creates that kind of emotion because it's such an intimate medium. It's the most intimate medium that there's ever been in the history of the world. There's no book that's ever been written that has the impact of TV. You get to know personally the people you're watching. Every trait comes through before it's all over, and you grow to love them in spite of their faults.

Fortunately for me, there was something in my little pudgy face that came across the TV screen in a positive way. The reason I know is that as the years went by, I seemed miraculously to have staying power in broadcasting.

The *Joy Boys* had gone off the air in 1972, and WRC had gradually done away with all the staff announcer positions. All the jobs I had once considered jewels in my crown had faded or fallen away, except one—my TV weather job.

As it turned out, it was the best and brightest treasure of all.

CHAPTER 13

Why It's Important
to Live in the Past

I'll admit it. I'm an idealist. I believe in Walt Disney, I want the world to be what I *think* it is, and I long for things to be the way they were.

In many ways it's true I'm a practical, pragmatic person. But in some areas of my life, I've tried to turn back the clock to recapture the joys of an earlier time when people's lives were rooted in the land. My little plot of nostalgia is a fifteen-acre farm in Virginia, which Mary and I bought about twenty years ago. While the girls were growing up, it was mainly a weekend and summer place. But about seven years ago we moved there permanently.

From the moment we bought it, though, the farm was much more to me than just a place to live. I saw it as a chance to re-create the happiness I had known as a kid on my grandfather's farm. Step by step, I started to build a farm just like my grandfather Phillips'—even down to the springhouse.

His springhouse had always meant so much to me that it was the very first building I put up on my own place. The day it was built, Herman and I had gone to Warrenton, Virginia, where I had appeared as Bozo at the opening of a shopping center. But the only thing on my mind that day was the springhouse.

As soon as the appearance was over, even without my bothering to change out of my Bozo costume, we jumped in the car and drove over to my little farm to see how things were going with the construction. The cement for the springhouse was still wet when we arrived, but that didn't stop us from going inside to soak up the atmosphere. We threw a few planks across the wet floor, then sat right down on the boards and pulled out a bottle of Early Times.

For both of us, that moment was a kind of communion with the past. For Herman, it was a communion with his father and grandfather because the springhouse represented the simple rural life they had lived down in North Carolina. For me, it was a link to Herman as we sat there together, and to my grandfather and my own childhood. To this day I make wine every fall and always go down to the springhouse and have a glass—"with Herman."

Little by little, the rest of the place was built. I put in a smokehouse like my grandfather's and started curing my own hams the way he taught me. I've always been a big ham myself; maybe that's why I got such a kick out of curing them, even as a kid.

Grandfather Phillips' smokehouse was a wood-frame

building with two rooms, one on the top floor that was like an attic, the other on the bottom floor where there was a big stone fireplace with a huge opening for smoking the hams. If you put that room in Greenwich Village today, it would probably rent for $5,000 a month as a quaint apartment.

My setup is very similar, and I follow his technique down to the last detail. Around about November, he'd make a little bench by putting three boards across a couple of sawhorses, and then he'd take some hams and lay them on top of the boards before he cured them.

There are two ways to cure ham: One is dry cure and the other is water cure in a salt solution. Grandfather Phillips always used a dry cure. That's the old Southern style. He would mix brown sugar, salt, pepper, saltpeter and spices. Then he'd cover the hams with this stuff and leave them on the boards, and every couple of weeks he'd go by and reapply the mixture.

He'd let the hams "cure out" like this for five or six weeks. After that, he'd scrub them and let them dry out for three or four days. Then, he'd take the hams up the creaky old steps to the top floor of the smokehouse, where he'd hang them on meathooks. Downstairs, he'd build a fire in the fireplace and close the flue so smoke would billow up. He'd smoke the hams for about a week to give them a nice flavor. Finally, he'd let the hams just hang there on the meathooks for about nine months. That's how you get a really good ham—by being patient.

There was nothing more exciting to me as a kid than to watch that smoke billow up, and then, after the smoking was done, to go into the smokehouse and see those hams just hanging there, getting more delicious day by day.

154

It was such a thrill that I cure my hams just like Grandfather did, except for one thing. He raised his own pigs and that was an awful lot of work. I get mine freshly killed from the butcher.

I really didn't intend for this to be a handbook on hams, but as I said, I'm obsessed with the subject. And I must say, I do darn good hams. I'm a lot better with them than with my weather forecasts. The hams are considerably more dependable!

Other than the smokehouse and the springhouse, though, my farm is a far cry from my grandfather's, and so is my lifestyle—there're no two ways about that. What it comes down to is that I have a gentleman's farm, and he had a *real* farm, one that was essential to his family's survival.

My house is anything but a classic, utilitarian farmhouse. It started out simply enough as a five-room Cape Cod, with stone walls and a cedar roof. We designed it from blueprints we bought for $25 out of a magazine. Gradually, though, we started tearing down walls and adding to it, until now it seems to spread all over the place. To top it off, we built a swimming pool out back.

Then there's my barn, which certainly wasn't made for honest labor. I didn't need a big old-fashioned barn like my grandfather's, since I never had any intention of raising cows. My barn is big enough for a couple of horses, a lot of cats, and a load of hay. The important thing to me is that it has that wonderful barnyard smell. When I walk into the barn, my nose is assaulted by the aroma of hay and horse manure, and I have the illusion of being a farmer, without the sweat.

My orchard, on the other hand, is much bigger and nicer than the one my grandfather had. He didn't have

time to take care of his, because he was too busy milking the cows and mowing hay. He and my grandmother simply picked whatever size apple nature gave them,
and ate it whether or not it was wormy or knotty. I'm
the kind of farmer who has nothing better to do than
take care of his orchard. I've got a hundred fruit trees
and there's not a wormy apple or peach in the bunch.

When I try to compare my life with my grandfather's,
I guess I'm living in fantasyland. I feel like a gangster
who's wearing twelve diamond rings and smoking
two-dollar cigars while he's talking about how wonderful it was back in the old country where seventeen
people lived in a one-room cabin. If somebody took me
back to my grandfather's farm right now, it would
probably seem strange if I had to be there more than a
night. I admit that I like all of the refinements of modern life.

But if it came down to a do-or-die choice, I'd take the
farm. There's an atmosphere in the country that goes
beyond the kind of house you live in or the number of
cows you have or the quality of your apples. This may
sound like something out of *Little House on the Prairie*,
but the fact is that on the farm there's an enthusiasm
about the little things in life.

Getting up and feeding the mule in the morning can
actually be an exciting experience. There's even joy in
oatmeal. Now, to most people oatmeal is just a bowl of
cereal. But to me, the very thought of making it and
eating it summons up a wealth of joyous memories of
country life. Ever since the kids were small, we had oatmeal at the farm, piping hot with fresh sausage on the
side. It was a ritual.

Not long ago I took my daughter Sally with me to the
Tournament of Roses Parade, and on the plane back

from California, I realized we didn't have any oatmeal in the house. So on the way home from the airport at 11:00 P.M., I found a store that would sell me some.

The next morning I bounced out of bed, headed for the kitchen, and put on a pot of coffee and some oatmeal. When it was ready, I yelled upstairs, "Sally, the oatmeal's ready!" And—boom—she came down the stairs.

Who can explain the excitement in a bowl of oatmeal? But to call upstairs, like you've done ever since your daughter was three years old, and to sit down together over a bowl of oatmeal, that's real, unadulterated joy.

I get that feeling about almost everything we do in the country. Everybody's got a project. Little Mary might be out in the barn taking care of her horse, while Sally is out feeding the dogs or the rabbit. As for Mary and me, we rarely sit still.

Just being on the farm makes life seem more fun. What's more, there's a freedom in the country that can't be duplicated anyplace else. What's so fantastic is the solitude and the privacy. It's knowing you can do anything you want to do without anyone looking over your shoulder. If you want to pee in the woods, you pee. That's the kind of freedom I'm talking about.

I feel this freedom most on rainy days. There's a kick sitting under the eaves of a barn just watching the water run off the roof and smelling the aroma of the water blending in with the horse manure. You don't think water has a fragrance? Try smelling it sometime on my farm.

Many's the time during a rain that I've gone down and sat with the cats—we have about fourteen of them hanging out at our barn. If nothing's going on in the house, I go down to the barn and open the latch and there's a nice wet smell of grain and manure. I'll sit there for a half hour or more all by myself. It's terrific.

Maybe the biggest joy of all I get from the country, though, is something so basic that even the cavemen shouted about it. Nothing has ever been as rewarding to me as providing food for my family. I mean *really* providing it: putting it in the ground as seeds, taking care of it, and harvesting it. But it means more to me than anything I've ever given my family—color TV sets, vacations, you name it. Nothing has given me more pleasure—absolutely nothing.

To give you an idea of what I'm talking about, let me tell you about the thrill you can get from something as simple as shelling peas. I don't like to *pick* peas because that's a laborious job. But shelling peas is something else. I'm like Grandma. I have a system. I go sit in the shade and spread out this little apron on my lap. On one side I have a bowl of peas in the pod, and on another I have a place to put the peas. Then I get a handful of pea pods and put them on my lap.

It's so nice to sit there under a tree, smoking my cigar or chewing my Beechnut or whatever, and having this little commune with nature and, in a very real sense, with Grandma as well.

Then, it gives me a special sense of accomplishment to look out over the dinner table and see a spread of fresh vegetables from my own garden: peas, cucumbers, lettuce, radishes, and potatoes, topped off with peaches from my own tree. It's beautiful, more beautiful than anything I've ever done.

That's why, no matter where I've been and whom I've seen—even if it's to London to see Lady Di, Prince

Charles, and the Queen—whenever I'm heading home to the farm, I get overcome with the excitement of anticipation as I draw closer to my own plot of land. It's the same feeling I remember as a kid of four or five, as we rounded the bend to Grandfather Phillips' farm. I was bubbling over with joy, my heart was pounding, and I couldn't wait to get there.

That incredible feeling is still there. It can be four o'clock in the morning, I'm heading toward the farm, and as soon as I hit the hill near home, I'm like a kid again. For a moment, at least, my life is the way it was.

But something is missing. My parents, Herman and Thelma, are gone.

CHAPTER 14

Stormy Weather for Willard

In the real world, a Walt Disney production doesn't always work out the way you want it to. For me, the fantasies started to crumble about ten years ago, when Herman and Thelma started to go downhill simultaneously.

Herman's problems had grown slowly over the years starting around the time I was in the Navy. I came home on leave after about six months, and for the first time I noticed that Herman seemed older. There was a look about him that I'd never seen before. He was talking about retiring and going on disability, which he did about a year later.

He had some emphysema, but the big problem was circulation. His legs hurt him all the time. Well, some of us thought it was because he drank too much.

Home-grown Silver Queen corn. *Photograph by Diana H. Walker/People Weekly.*

My mother and father. *Photograph courtesy of James Weaver.*

Ronald McDonald from the ground up. *Photograph by Diana H. Walker / People Weekly.*

The smart, cool First Lady and friend. *Photograph by JEB (Joan E. Biren).*

They were supposed to be pre-shrunk jeans! *Photograph by Diana H. Walker/ People Weekly.*

Our livestock: Tony the Pony, Roberta the Burro and one of our fourteen cats. *Photograph by Diana H. Walker/People Weekly.*

Doing the weather for the Arthritis Foundation. *Photograph courtesy of the Arthritis Foundation.*

The other family. Chris Wallace, Gene Shalit, Jane Pauley and Bryant Gumbel. *NBC photograph.*

But unbeknown to all of us, it was the beginning of a serious weakness in his aorta, the artery leading to the heart. The artery walls had weakened, and little by little the blood was slowing down as it pumped through his system. By 1972, the problem had gotten so bad that his aorta almost ruptured. He had an aneurism—a ballooning of the artery wall.

Luckily, the old family doctor, Walter Nalls, pulled Herman through. Herman went through a four-hour operation and was in intensive care for about two weeks. The worst part about the whole operation, though, was his gut-wrenching agony of being off booze for all that time.

About three days after the operation, I went into the intensive care unit and noticed that my father was jerking, shaking, and babbling a lot. I thought it was the medicine he was taking. But the doctor had another explanation.

"Your father's going through the DTs," he said.

I couldn't accept it. "C'mon, Doc," I said. "You don't have to lie to me. If y'all screwed up in the operating room, let's be honest and talk about it. I'm not going to sue you."

But the doctor held his ground. "He's going through the DTs, I tell you."

"My father never drank that much," I protested. But finally, I realized the doctor was absolutely right. Herman had been drinking on a regular basis since he was about eighteen years old, and now he was in intensive care. For two weeks he was almost unconscious.

It was kind of a shocker for me to see something like that happening to my own father. It must have shocked Herman, too, because after that he never drank another drop until the last six months of his life. But by then he had really lost the taste for it.

161

But even though Herman was aging before my eyes, Thelma never seemed to change physically. She was always a beautiful woman, even as she grew older. Her problem was much more subtle. Little by little, starting around about the time Herman had his aorta problems, Thelma began acting kind of funny.

One Thanksgiving in particular, she did something I'd never seen her do before. We were sitting there at the table, and she actually took her teeth out at the table. I was so embarrassed for her. But I didn't say anything until the next day.

"Mother, what was the matter with you over Thanksgiving?" I asked on the phone.

"What do you mean?" she said.

"You took your teeth out at the table."

She didn't remember one thing about it. That's when it started to dawn on me that something was radically wrong. Gradually, Thelma became more and more forgetful. She would come down in the morning and fix breakfast like she'd been doing all her life, and she'd turn on the coffee pot and forget to put the coffee in it.

At other times, she'd fill in her checkbook and forget to keep track of the amounts. Since she'd always been a very methodical person, her behavior was puzzling, and one day I got a little hard on her.

"Mother, don't you know how to fill in your checkbook? You've been writing checks for years."

She started to cry. "I don't know what's the matter," she said. "I just can't get it right."

Two years later her illness came on like a house afire. It was called Alzheimer's Disease, and it was caused by the premature death of nerve cells throughout the brain. The effect was devastating: A robust, healthy woman, still in her sixties, was rapidly growing senile.

For a while, Herman and Thelma were able to take care of each other in their row house in Alexandria, where they had been since 1939. I'd go over every night between weather forecasts to check up on them and to say hello. But gradually it became clear to me that Herman was so limited and Thelma was in such bad shape that they needed someone in to help them every day.

Before long, we had people taking care of them around the clock. But the place soon turned into a three-ring circus. Mother was half out of her mind, and Herman was fit to be tied having all these nurses under foot. He was not only physically sick, but on top of that he was just losing his patience. Of course, he never had much patience anyway. But for a proud, independent guy like Herman, having to depend on people drove him nuts.

He reached the point where he was throwing people out of the house right and left and raising the dickens. At three o'clock in the morning I'd get calls from the night nurse saying, "I can't stand it. This man is driving me crazy."

And in the background I'd hear Herman cussing up a storm. "Get out of this house before I bust your head open," he'd scream at the nurse.

Then I'd get him on the phone and try to smooth things over. "Herman, calm down. I'll be over the first chance I get."

For a few minutes, at least, Herman would repent. "I don't want to mess up your life, boy," he'd say.

Moments later, though, he'd be up to his tricks, and I'd have to drive over to make peace or stay the night with him because he'd thrown a nurse out.

163

After a while it began to wear on me, like battle fatigue. I was going over every night between shows, along with being waked up by phone calls in the middle of the night and then having to drive nearly an hour to Herman and Thelma's.

As if the problems with the nurses weren't enough, Herman and Thelma were going at each other like cats and dogs. Thelma had been docile all her life, but once her mind started to go, she got feisty and fought Herman tooth and nail. The two of them would go round and round like those cats in the cartoons. It was constant conflict.

I was exhausted, and I finally realized I had to make some hard decisions. One option was to put Mother in a nursing home. I had checked into two or three of them, and I had the typical reaction that everyone has the first time they visit. "My mother will *never* go into one of these, I'll never do that to her," I told myself.

But there was another alternative close at hand. We had a cabin up at the farm—it was more like a little house, really. It had a big living room, a little bedroom in the back, a bathroom, and a kitchen. It also had a nice stone fireplace.

At the time, it seemed like Herman and Thelma could be comfortable there. They could be near us, so we could keep tabs on them, and we could have some local people they knew come in to help out and cook for them. So right after Christmas, in 1976, up to the country they went, leaving behind their old row house in Alexandria and a lifetime of memories for all of us.

The day they moved, Herman and I stood on the stoop together in Alexandria, and I let him shut the door to the house and lock it for the last time. I remember watching his hands. They were old and brown, with broken veins, and he sort of fumbled with the key. He had a little sweatball on his nose, and he was shaking as he turned the key in the lock.

Perhaps he was thinking, as I was, of all the things that had happened on that front stoop. I remembered my eighth birthday and how it had just snowed and all the kids came running up that little set of stoops to my party inside. Then there was the time I slammed the front door and got my finger caught in it. Mother came out and fixed it up, and about twenty minutes later, I went back out again and slipped on the stoop, skinning my leg and ripping my pants.

It was on that stoop, too, that I first heard that Roosevelt had died. Herman and I had been to Washington to buy an eight-dollar pair of shoes. We didn't have a radio in the car, and when we got back from shopping, Mother was standing at the door. As we walked up the stoop, she gave us the news about the President. Herman had been a staunch Democrat all his life, so Roosevelt's death had a big impact on him.

So much of our lives, it seemed, had taken place in that spot. At Christmas, it had always been my job to decorate the front door. We had a wreath along with a little ring of lights I placed around it. The front door was also the place where Thelma and I waited for Herman to take us to the country every weekend. He'd be at the dairy getting juiced up with the boys, and we'd be looking out the front door, waiting for Herman to come up the front stoop to take us to Maryland.

Now, here I was, taking Herman up to the country for a very different reason. It seemed so natural to leave the house that day, like we were just going for a short trip. But Herman was leaving it forever.

After that, we cleaned out the house and rented it out

165

to help pay for Herman and Thelma's care. The only thing of theirs left in the place was a broken pantry key. At some point over the years, part of the key had broken off, and as I was going through their things, I came across it. I remembered how it had sat in that pantry door for years, and somehow it didn't seem right to throw it out. So I took the key and hid it up under the eaves in the basement. Only I know where it is. Nobody else would ever find it unless they tore the house apart.

That key is the very last vestige of our lives together. Even when I walk in that house today, I walk down into the basement to touch the key—and remember.

Once Herman and Thelma got up to the cabin on our farm, we tried to make it as nice as we could for them. They had made many wonderful friends up in the country over the years when they visited us, and now that they were in the cabin permanently, there was a lot of visiting back and forth. Herman would go around and see the old folks and have coffee with them. Then his friends would bring over apples and homemade butter.

An old family friend, Leola, stayed with them and cooked just the way Herman liked, crispy bacon and cornbread and grits. Then there were some sweet old country people who came in to help every day, giving them baths and dressing them and cleaning up. A couple of times a week we'd have them up to the house for dinner, and often Little Mary and Sally would go over to visit.

We all pitched in to make things go smoothly. I'd come over sometimes and do their toenails. That's something you just can't do for yourself when you get old. I wonder how many sweet old people are sitting around now who don't feel that bad except for their feet? Their feet may be killing them because their nails are so ingrown, and that's because no one's cut them in years. I did it for Herman and Thelma because it was one of the little ways I could really show love and care for them.

Also, one night when no one else was around to help, I gave Herman a bath. The poor old guy shook pretty bad, but somehow I managed to bathe him and towel him off. Was that ever a switch.

I may have managed Herman's bath without too many problems, but I didn't do quite as well helping Thelma to the toilet. With her mind gone, she'd go to the bathroom but then she'd immediately stand up before she finished her business. I was in there with her one day, and when I saw what she was doing, I said, "Wait—you've got to sit there while I help you take care of things."

I held her shoulders to keep her down on the pot, but she wouldn't be restrained. She pushed up and I pushed down, and before I knew it I had pushed her a little too hard. Her back hit the back of the toilet, and she grabbed her side and started moaning.

It turned out that I had broken her rib—right there on the toilet—the spot where that same sweet woman had once spent hours rocking me to sleep as a child.

Life in the little cabin might have gone smoothly if Herman's and Thelma's fights hadn't gotten worse and worse. It was a battle royal, and all of us became victims of their passion at one time or another. Once we were in Arizona and got a call from Little Mary. She had stopped in to see them and Herman had knocked her down. He adored her, but he had gotten so agitated he went out of his head. He had pushed her aside in a fit of anger over something or other.

I couldn't hate him for it. I knew he wasn't himself.

Nothing made him happy. He had everything he could ever want. He was well cared for, and he was surrounded by people who really loved him. But he was just old and tired and ready to die.

Ater about six months of this "togetherness" in the country, Thelma was pretty far gone and was screaming so much at Herman that we finally had to do what I vowed never to do: put her in a nursing home. I just ran out of rope after a while.

We found a lovely home over in the Shenandoah Valley. But even though it was nice, no place is ever nice enough for your own mother. The first day I took her over we left after an hour. The floors had been cleaned with Lysol and the place was really spotless. But Mother always had a great nose on her face, and she could smell *anything*. She may not have understood what was happening to her, but she could smell that Lysol and she let me know she didn't like it one bit.

I couldn't take it. So I packed her up and brought her home. Finally, Mary had to take her back the next day.

The staff at the nursing home were terrific. They were so in love with her, and they kept her looking nice. She had a lady in the room with her who she thought was her mother, so she was happy. On Wednesdays and Sundays she came home to visit Herman, but after about five minutes, they'd start cussing each other out.

Back at the nursing home, though, Mother was a different person. Even in the state she was in, she still had a quiet, giving way about her, and people responded to her immediately. There were a couple of people in there who just doted on her. An old white man and an old black man in particular walked her around the halls because they were just crazy about her.

That's the way it was in that nursing home. People looked after each other. If one lady was totally bedridden, another old lady in a wheelchair would roll over and make sure she got her last bite of Jell-O. Every time I visited, I saw dozens of examples of quiet inspiration like that. It isn't the kind of thing you read about in the newspapers or in *People* magazine, because it isn't glamorous or chic. But it drew me to those people and made me grow to love them like my own family.

Whenever I'd go to visit Mother, I'd play the role of an old Baptist preacher. I always had my rounds to make, visiting about fifteen or twenty old folks. I'd pat them on the head, give them a glass of water, or grab their toe, just like in the Bozo days.

As for Thelma, I tried everything I could to make her life seem normal. We even threw her a birthday party—her seventy-third—on October 5, 1977. On my way to work that day, I brought her a birthday cake that Leola had made for her. It was a triple-layer coconut cake. I rounded up a few "guests"—an old lady from the next room, another in the bed next to Mother who could barely speak, and an old man in a wheelchair.

Mother was aware of the cake and she mentioned how pretty it was, but I don't even know if she knew it was her birthday. That's how bad her condition was at that point.

Meanwhile, Herman was in even worse shape. He had experienced a severe series of intestinal problems and ended up in a hospital for nearly two months.

Because I could sense that both of them were close to the end, I decided to give Herman a real bang-up homecoming from the hospital by getting him and Mother together at the cabin one last time. I planned the meeting down to the last detail so that everything would be perfect. My uncle, Guy Scott, went to get Herman at the hospital. I picked up Thelma at the nursing home, where the staff had dressed her up in a pretty dress, put some jewelry on her, and fixed her hair. She looked lovely.

As Thelma and I waited for Herman in the cabin, having tea and crackers by the fire, she was quiet and calm. The whole scene was so nice and peaceful that I thought maybe this time would be different. Maybe today we could have a nice cozy get-together around the fire, holding hands and smiling at each other.

But as I said, Walt Disney doesn't always work out in real life. When Herman arrived, he looked like he was at death's door. It took him a half hour to get from Guy Scott's car into the house. He put one foot in front of the other and shuffled into the cabin, staring blankly into space.

Thelma took one look at Herman, and walked over and socked him one. "I hate you, you S.O.B.," she screamed.

She kept yelling as I hustled her off to the car to take her back to the nursing home.

As I drove Mother away from the cabin, I began to cry. I had wanted so much for them to hug each other. I had wanted a happy ending, wth birds singing, heavenly choirs humming, the whole bit. But as I said, Walt Disney doesn't always work out.

It was the last time they saw each other alive.

A week later, Mother died, and just thirty-six days after that Herman was gone, too. Overnight, it seemed, I had lost both of my parents.

It was the greatest tragedy of my life.

What made the loss even greater for me was that I wasn't even present during their last moments. The week Mother died, I had been called twice by the nursing home to say that she was close to death and that I should come right down. I had rushed over, and each time she had rallied.

So when I got another call on Friday, November 3, at 4:00 P.M., it didn't seem like an emergency. I asked the doctor, "If I leave now, I'll get there by six-thirty. If I do my weather show, I'll get there around seven-thirty. What do you think?"

"Seven-thirty will be fine," said the doctor.

After my show, I walked into the nursing home and this sweet old man whom I had visited often grabbed my hand. "I'm sorry about your mother," he said.

"Is she dead?" I asked.

"You didn't know?" he said sadly. "I'm so sorry."

I went into her room and walked up to the bed. Slowly, the nurse pulled down the sheet, and I looked at Mother's face. But what I saw wasn't the face of an old woman who had slowly lost her mind.

Instead, saw a vision of Mother as a young, robust woman, and me as a child in the bathroom of our house in Alexandria. She was sitting on the lid of the toilet seat, holding me on her lap. Her arms were hugging me tight, and she was rocking me to sleep singing Brahms' lullaby.

Even in death, Thelma was still giving me comfort.

We took Mother back to the old First Baptist Church in Alexandria for her funeral. It was like we were bringing her home. She had loved that church so much, and everybody had loved her. One lady in her nineties, Mrs. Barrett, who had taught her in Sunday School, even came to the funeral.

Right before the funeral, I walked into the cabin to pick up Herman, and over on the couch I spotted the Teddy bear Thelma had given me when I was about six

171

months old. That bear had just sort of hung around all these years because Thelma had loved it. She had it in Alexandria, and had sewn up the hand when the cotton came out and had put another eye back in. For some strange reason, the bear had ended up in the cabin.

I took the bear and stuck it in a little pillowcase and brought it with me to the church. When I walked up to the casket to say my last goodbyes, I slipped it out of the pillowcase and placed it in her arms.

I don't know why I did it. It was just one of those things that seemed to make sense at the time. But what touched me most of all was Little Mary's reaction. As we drove home that day, she was crying and she leaned over and kissed me. "Dad, that was the sweetest thing I've ever seen."

As for Herman, he had looked like a cadaver walking down the church aisle at the funeral, and afterwards, he just wasn't the same. He refused to have anybody in the cabin with him during the day. "It would drive me crazy," he said. We had somebody come in at night to fix meals for him, and I left a bottle of whiskey down there hoping he'd have a couple of drinks and get his appetite back. He had a drink or two, but he didn't seem to enjoy it much.

The old Herman was gone, completely gone—except for the day we tried to buy him a new suit. Little Mary had a school Christmas concert coming up, and we wanted the whole family to be there. The trouble was, Herman had nothing decent to wear. He had lost so much weight from his illness that his old suit had hung funny on him at Mother's funeral.

A couple of weeks later, I said to him, "Let's go over to Winchester and get you a new suit. You've got to go to Little Mary's concert and you don't want to look like you're about to be embalmed."

Over his protests, we packed him into the car and headed to a nearby store. It took four of us to control him—Leola, Little Mary, Sally, and me.

I was the advance man. I ran into the store and said, "My father's here, he's in bad shape, he's old, and he's cantankerous. Get me a suit as fast as you can. Stick it on him, put cuffs and whatever he wants on it, and let me get out of here."

As soon as he walked in, he started cussing. But within fifteen minutes they had a suit on him, off him, tailored, and in the bag and off we went.

He wore it only once. He was laid away in it at his own funeral the next week. He looked terrific, and he would have been proud.

The day he died, Mary and I were at a wedding in the District. When we left that morning, everything seemed to be going fine. In fact, Herman had been acting a little more like himself for the past few days. He wasn't exactly kicking up his heels, but every now and then he'd take a little turn in the garden, and people would come by to see him. He even managed to pack away some raw oysters I brought him, and a man can't be too sick to eat raw oysters.

When we left for the wedding, I told him, "Herman, we're going to town. The girls are going to be here off and on, so they'll check up on you. I'll see you before we go to bed."

Then I gave him a hug. We always hugged. I kissed him on the forehead, patted him on the shoulder, and said goodbye. I didn't know it would be for the last time.

When I called home after the wedding to see how he was, the line was busy. Five minutes later Little Mary answered the phone in tears.

She had found him dead in the cabin. Herman had gone out on the porch about 3:00 P.M. and hollered for her to go to the store and get him some buttermilk. He was going to make himself some buttermilk and cornbread mush that *his* father had loved so much back in North Carolina.

Well, Mary had gone to the store and lolligagged and didn't get back for an hour. She walked in and found him slumped over in the chair.

He was seventy-two when he died. Mother had just turned seventy-three. It would have embarrassed her to death because she hated anyone to know that she was a few months older than Herman. We buried them together over in National Memorial Park, and to this day I go over a couple of times a year to pay my respects.

In the end, though, I came away with a kind of joy that I never thought possible after such a tragedy. I understood what the Psalmist meant when he wrote, "Weeping may tarry for the night, but joy comes with the morning." (Psalms 30:5, RSV)

For me, the joy came from what I call the "honesty factor": following the basic code of love and affection and sincerity and being true to myself and my past.

I believe there's more guilt on the part of people today who have allowed their parents to go down the chute. But to bury your parents with no regrets is to me one of the most rewarding things that you can do for yourself.

Harry Truman summed it up best when he described

an old tombstone in Arizona. It read: "Here lies Jack Davis—he done his damndest."

To me, that's what joy is all about, doing your best for your family, your friends, your job, and for God.

Down South we have another word for it—it's called duty. And there's no one who understood the word better than another one of my heroes, General Robert E. Lee.

CHAPTER 15

Duty Isn't a Dirty Word

I'm a closet Confederate, not in the sense of yearning for a life of privilege in a columned house on a hill, but because of the people. I was raised to revere those people and the ideals and heroes that stirred them.

In my hometown, Alexandria, we had a statue of a Confederate soldier right in the center of town. He still stands there, even though many groups have tried to get rid of him over the years. What's saved him, I think, is that he's not an aggressor. He doesn't even carry a gun. He's simply got his hat in his hand and he's looking south, toward "home."

I've always regretted that a lot of people in the rest of the country think of us Southerners as a bunch of hillbilly red-neck bigots who are set in their ways, and run around with gunracks on the back of their pickup trucks. There's some of that, of course. But there's much more to the South than things like grits and redeye gravy and country ham.

The real South, the South I know and love, is the South of General Robert E. Lee. I come from a school that teaches you should have someone to pattern your life after. And next to Jesus himself, there's no one I'd rather follow than Lee. So many people have misunderstood what Lee means to a real Southerner. They think of him as leading the great Gray line into battle and the marvelous victories and the disastrous defeats.

To my way of thinking, though, Lee embodied the qualities of refinement and nobility that represented the best of the Old South. He lived by an almost chivalrous code of honor, according to which a man's word was his only contract, honesty meant something, and duty wasn't considered a dirty word. All his life Lee conducted himself in such a way as to bring honor upon himself and the people he loved around him.

Most people don't realize it, but at the beginning of the War Between the States, Lee was offered the command of the Union Army by Lincoln. The President offered it to him not only because Lee was a very respected soldier, but also because it was wise politically. If Lee had become the commander of the Union Army it might have been more difficult for his home state of Virginia to secede. It would certainly have caused a lot of problems in the South because Lee came from a traditional Southern family.

Lee, of course, turned Lincoln down. He refused the command and resigned his commission in the United States Army where he had an outstanding record. He stayed with the South, because his first duty was to his family, and he considered the whole state of Virginia his family.

He didn't come from a wealthy family. His father was a bad businessman who had lost almost everything. After his father died, Lee lived with his mother in a nice little house in Alexandria. Then he went to West Point and was in the Army and traveled all over the country. He fought in the Mexican War and was in the St. Louis Corps of Engineers. One of his jobs was chief engineer on a project to build the levees along the Mississippi that are still there holding back the flood waters.

Later, he married the Custis girl who was Martha Washington's great-granddaughter. Her family had slaves over in Arlington, but Lee himself was never for slavery. He never owned a slave in his life. Many think the Civil War was fought for and against slavery, and that every Southerner was for slavery. But Lee's loyalty to the South was simply out of a sense of duty.

After the war, his sense of duty led him to pledge allegiance to the Union and devote his life to service. He went down to Lexington, Virginia, and became president of Washington College, a poor, faltering institution that later became Washington and Lee. There he worked to train a generation of Southerners in the noble ideals he cherished.

In a word, Lee was an aristocrat. He had that certain style and grace that comes with being a true gentleman. I'm not sure I'm 100 percent for bringing back an aristocracy to America, but I do believe there's something to be learned from true aristocrats, code-of-honor-type people whom you can look up to because they affirm a high standard of values.

Being a non-aristocrat myself, I can say all this with impunity. Our family was a bunch of dirt farmers. But there's a part of me that goes for gentility and breeding. I'm basically a peasant who would like to be knighted or made a lord or something like that.

While I like to sit around in my T-shirt in front of a fireplace and drink a beer, I also enjoy and feel uplifted by the decorum of a refined place like the Episcopal church near my farm in Virginia. I like going through communion and morning prayers and shaking hands with the priest. I like going to somebody's house after church and having a biscuit with a little piece of ham in the middle of it and a glass of bourbon. And I like being around a lovely home with old pictures and beautiful silver and people who may or may not be boring but who are nice and gracious and don't swear.

Of course, if the ham and biscuits and bourbon were all there was to this aristocracy business, it wouldn't be worth emulating. But underneath the formality there's a tradition that smacks of something noble, of people like Lee and of characters like Melanie in *Gone With the Wind*.

I saw that movie when it was first produced and I see it every time it comes back. But as I've grown older my heroes in the movie have changed. When I was a kid, my hero was Ashley. I thought he was just wonderful, but it turned out that he was tremendously weak. As I got a little older, I identified with Rhett Butler. The last time I saw *Gone With the Wind*, though, I realized that for me the true star of the movie was Melanie. More than any other character, she epitomized the good and noble qualities of a Southern aristocrat. She knew that Scarlett O'Hara was hot for her husband, Ashley. And she probably knew that he lusted after her and that there was a lot of hanky-panky going on. Yet never once did she accuse or butt in.

She knew she was living by the rules, by the old code

of honor which demanded that you put duty to family first. As a result, she could bear her burden nobly and joyfully, knowing that she had done the right thing.

In my own small way, I pay homage to the code of honor of the Old South on General Lee's birthday, January 19. We have a little dinner party and invite about twenty people for a traditional Virginia dinner. There's country ham that we smoke ourselves, and usually a grits dish—not just plain grits, but something fancy like cheese grits or grits soufflé. Then there's peanut soup and pecan pie. On the table are little Confederate flags and red and white carnations. Afterwards, one of the guests will read Lee's farewell to his troops.

We don't get all misty-eyed and say a prayer to bless the South or salute the Confederate flag; it's not that kind of occasion. The whole thing is done a little bit out of tradition, and a little bit out of fun. It's also done a little bit out of the fact that January 19 is three weeks after Christmas and two weeks after New Year's and January is a terribly dull, boring month. Lee's birthday is a great rallying point to get your spirits soaring.

For me, the day is also a reminder of something to strive for. I'd like to be like Lee. I'd like to be as much of a gentleman as he was. I'd like to be as honorable. I'd like to be as loyal, and I'd like to have as much of a sense of duty as he did.

A guy like Lee wasn't looking out for number one. He was looking out for everybody else, and his life made a difference. He chose to do his duty first, and he was paid back in overwhelming adoration from his family, his troops, and even his enemies.

What I'm talking about isn't just some pie-in-the-sky ideal you read etched in marble about some guy who has been dead more than 120 years. It has practical implications for how you live your life right now and what you really are going to get out of it.

Where we've really gone off the beam today is in turning our backs on our responsibilities to our jobs and to our families. The result is that the joy of living has gone out of our lives.

Take work, for example. General Lee was the kind of guy who put 100 percent into a job, whether it was leading the Confederate troops or heading up a small, struggling college. His philosophy of work was a lot like that of my grandfather Phillips, who used to tell me, "Willard, do it *right*, or not at all."

But that philosophy of work seems to have gone by the boards these days. Today, people are part of what I like to call the "car wash" generation. Before World War II, when you wanted your car washed, you took it to a service station, paid a buck and a half, and the service station would spend an hour and a half washing your car. Sixteen people would swarm all over it to clean it, wax it, and polish the chrome on the inside with a toothbrush. To finish it off, when they got to the hubcaps with the word "Dodge" engraved on them, they'd use their fingernail to clean all the wax out of the letters.

After the war, things changed. The first car washes were introduced, and they seemed wonderful, at least on the surface. You drove in and what used to take an hour and a half now took three minutes. The car was all shiny, except you weren't supposed to look underneath the fenders or examine the chrome. If you did, you'd see that the whole thing was an absolute mess. The job was totally inadequate.

We've all sort of gotten that way. Everything today is "let's get by with what we can." These days you see the cars go through the car wash and the guy at the finishing line takes a towel, slaps the car with it once, and says, "That'll be five dollars." The ashtrays haven't even been cleaned.

Not only do we do a slipshod job at work, we also give short shrift to our families. We've become so wrapped up in ourselves these days that we have broken faith with those we love, particularly our kids. The result is that instead of getting joy out of life, we become cynical.

Consider what happens to a guy who goes to see his son appear as Humpty-Dumpty in the kindergarten play. The guy goes because he knows it's his obligation, but he's not convinced it's worth it.

A few years later, when the kid's in an elementary school play, the father goes again, but this time he starts shifting in his seat and grumbling, "When will this thing be over?" When the junior high play comes up, the father begs off with a lame excuse. "I really can't go this time."

By the time of the kid's high school play, the father has come full circle, from a sense of duty and responsibility to total selfishness. "I just don't want to go to the play," he tells his son.

At this point the man has become a cynic and in effect blames the kid for intruding on his life. What the guy has really done, however, is betray his own basic, innate feelings. He's gone against the code of honor that is written on each of our hearts. And what he's lost in the process is the fun he would have had just sitting back and enjoying his kid's play. The joy is there for the asking.

What it all boils down to is that you *can* bring the joy back in life by living a life you can be proud of. Now, you don't need Robert E. Lee to set the standard for your life. But we all need a model, or a guide, to give us confidence that we are on the right track.

There's an old country song I love that compares life to a mountain railroad. The idea of the song is that a mountain railroad is twisty and turny and if you don't stay right on the tracks and watch every move and every turn, you could open the throttle at the wrong turn and the whole thing could go right down the side of the hill.

That song rings true to me because I know there's really only one way to stay on the right track in life. And that's to follow the greatest Engineer of all time. His principles for keeping on track are laid down in a handy how-to book that's so simple, so honest, and so "square" that most folks don't consider it relevant to these complicated and perilous times we live in.

And yet this book has been around for quite some time. It has the answers to every problem you will ever have in this life or—and here's the part that's really tough for some people to swallow—in the *next* life. The basic theme of this book is love, and it's all about giving and receiving which is what love is all about.

Chances are that you have a copy of this basic how-to manual somewhere within your reach at this moment. If not, turn the page and let me give you a poor substitute: the Gospel According to St. Willard.

CHAPTER 16

Faith Is a Package Plan

Over the years, I've made lots of personal appearances. I made them for twenty-five years in the Washington area, and now I'm getting requests to make speeches and personal appearances all over the country. I do about twenty or thirty a year. At the end of every talk, there's one question that always seems to pop up in groups all over the country.

"What makes you so happy?" people ask. "Where do you get your sunny disposition?"

Now, even though my response is sometimes met with silence or uneasiness by the audience, my honest answer is this: I'm happy and joyful because I believe in Jesus Christ and his teachings. I am a practicing Christian. I believe in life after death. I know that my sins (and there have been many) have been forgiven. I simply say that a religion that offers me salvation, forgiveness, and eternal life can't help but mold my personality and my outlook on life.

I realize that when you talk religion or politics you are treading on sacred—and controversial—ground. And I in no way wish to force my religious convictions on others. But when the question is asked, as it always is, I can only respond by giving the same honest answers.

I also say honestly that I've been blessed with a lot of good breaks in this world. I've had lots of love, a good home, good health, and a successful career. But I also know that, in the last analysis, my faith is my ultimate strength.

So, I want my light to shine. I want to brighten the corner where I am. And I much prefer to let people see what I am before I tell them. Perhaps the only subtle thing in my life is that I always wait to give the answer to that question about the source of my happiness only after it's asked.

I'm a Christian 100 percent. I happen to think that Christianity is the gentlest religion in the world, because its message is love.

Don't ask me what love is. Love is love. If you have to ask what it is—if you don't feel it—then you don't have it. I'm sick of people who say "Let's analyze it, let's dissect it, let's put it under a microscope and cut it till there's nothing left of it." If you do that to love, you've missed it.

The Christian faith is very simple. It's basically a matter of family love. The whole religion is summed up in a verse I could recite since I was knee-high to a grasshopper, John 3:16: "For God loved the world so much

185

that he gave his only Son, so that everyone who believes in him may not die but have eternal life." (TEV)

The thing that hits home to me about that verse is that God gave a part of his own *family* to save the world. I mean, he gave up his very own *son* so that the rest of us could be forgiven for whatever it was that we did wrong and become part of God's loving family, too.

What's more, God left a loophole big enough to put a truck through so that *anyone* could be part of his family. The way he set up the deal, even the worst, most horrible criminal offender could in the end turn and make peace with God. That's ultimate love. That's forgiveness.

To get in on this deal, you don't have to own one single thing. You don't have to have a ticket; you don't have to save green stamps. It's not possible to buy your way in. All you have to do to be part of God's family is give your heart and your soul and your mind to him. All you have to do is *believe.*

You can't believe only part of it, though. The thing about Christianity is that you have to buy the package plan. That's what we call it in broadcasting. It's not like a Chinese menu where you take one from Column A and one from Column B and forget the soup. You have to buy the whole deal. If you don't believe it all, forget it. I don't care if you don't understand how Mary conceived without a man or how Jesus performed his miracles. Who gives a rat's tail *how* it happened. It happened, and that's that.

My great moment of truth, when I finally bought the package plan, came when I was in my thirties. That's when I stopped trying to come up with all the answers and realized that the secret to the whole thing is faith.

Christianity can't be outlined and explained in neat little compartments. The whole point is that it's a mystery that will finally be unraveled when we meet the Master face to face. But here on earth, after you have the faith, the striving is everything. It's what you put into it that counts.

To me, the Christian faith is a little bit like the Yellow Brick Road to Oz. Do you remember what happened to the Tin Man and the Lion in *The Wizard of Oz*? They had started out toward Oz in search of courage and compassion, hoping that the Wizard would give it to them. But when they stood up before the magnificent and wonderful Wizard, all he gave them was a piece of paper and a little old tin heart. The courage and compassion they had been searching for had actually been developing inside them on the Yellow Brick Road through the course of their quest.

Christianity is somewhat like that. By having faith in that tremendous goal of perfect love that God set forth through his son, Jesus, we get power to give more love to others than we ever thought possible. By simply accepting God's word at face value, we have access to the most obvious source of personal power in the whole world. It's the power that gives your life dignity and happiness and produces peace in your heart. *Everybody* can plug into it, but most people totally ignore it. Maybe it's *too* simple.

It's so obvious, everyone misses the point completely. It's like an old vaudeville routine I used to do as Bozo the Clown. Bozo would come on stage, and a gorilla would hide behind him, aping his every move. All the kids in the audience knew the gorilla was there, and they would scream and yell at Bozo trying to tell him to turn around to see it. But Bozo couldn't understand what all the commotion was about.

"What's the matter?" he would ask. Then he'd walk to one side of the stage, and the gorilla would follow right behind him.

"He's behind you," the kids would shout, trying frantically to give him the message.

But Bozo still missed the point. He'd grin at the kids and say, "Yuk yuk," and keep clowning around as though nothing were wrong.

The ape was there on the stage all the time, but Bozo never did find him.

In real life, too, the very thing people are looking for and need is there for the asking. To find it, all you have to do is walk in anywhere—a closet, a bathroom, a church—and drop to your knees and say, "Here I am, God, do with me as you will. I believe I love you. I *know* you love me. You won't steer me wrong. I can do it now. You can help me do it."

But a lot of people are either too proud or too scared to take this step. We think we're so enlightened, sophisticated, advanced, and clever that we don't need anybody but ourselves. We don't believe there's anything that we can't do or that can't be done for us through technology or chemistry.

We spend millions of dollars for medical research, but not one iota for any research on how the kind of faith I'm talking about affects man's mind, body, and spirit.

How many half-sick people are walking around who only need one medicine to get well: a shot of "Dr. Jesus." He was the one person in all of history who showed us all how we could get the most out of life. What he preached wasn't a namby-pamby little goody-two-shoes message that is only good for Sunday and your new Sears' suit. He wasn't talking about some life in the future where you'll be by and by. He was talking about your everyday life, here and now.

His whole thing was people, and how to relate to them. He showed us that the opportunity to show love is everywhere. It's there in the nursing home with your grandfather who is waiting to die; it's there with your boss, your wife, your kids. And it's there with the woman at the checkout counter in the grocery store.

My image of Jesus is completely opposite from the way he's depicted in the movies. Somehow, he's always an ethereal, emaciated soul with an incredible wild-eyed look who kind of floats around with a flowing robe around him.

I see him as a big man, a very giving, physical person. My Jesus is more like Robert Morley, the jovial British actor who does commercials. The way I picture him, he'd probably yell, and he'd like jokes. Maybe he was short and kind of balding. All I know is, he was a real outgoing guy.

He loved parties and always showed up. If he walked on earth today he'd probably be on the *Today Show* because he used every vehicle of his time to reach people. He showed up at the temple, the marketplace, and the well, which in those days was the place where you could meet everybody in town.

He was show-biz. Once he was ready to reveal himself to the world, he rarely did anything in secret. He raised Lazarus from the dead in front of a whole town, not in a closet somewhere.

The way I see it, Jesus must have had something awfully good to sell, because nobody would have left a good carpentry job to go out and walk the streets for nothing! He must have had something he thought everybody would be hot to get hold of.

But like most folks today, many of the people in Jesus' time thought he would have been better off building cabinets. They weren't interested in what he had to offer, even though they needed it desperately.

Now, suppose he had tried the hard sell and put a fat price tag on his product, guaranteeing delivery of salvation, offering life after death, and promising to wipe out all the problems of the world. People would probably be falling all over themselves to sign on the dotted line! All these women in their fur coats and $7,000 Gucci bags and the guys with the diamond pinky rings would be standing in line to get in on the deal.

But Jesus was giving it away for free. What he was trying to tell us—and still is—is that God is offering us a great deal. I mean, God made this fantastic world and everything in it. He's given us 7-Elevens, Big Macs, and the Superbowl. He's given us everything, and all he asks in return is that we stay away from a few cookie jars. In other words, all he asks is that we live by a few simple rules that are set up not as a punishment, but as a way to reach inner peace.

To me, it's all summed up in the First Commandment: "You shall have no other Gods before me." That's the only one of the Ten Commandments that is really worth anything. The others are all things that you do when you're out of whack with the first one.

But putting God first in your life—before money, power, fame, and anything else you hold dear—is the greatest challenge of all. It also brings the greatest rewards. When you make God number one, you are acknowledging a source of power greater than you. In return you get the incredible strength of knowing you're not alone.

Now, you may argue that God's rules were made for a

190

nomadic people who lived two million years ago and don't apply today. But I say they're just as true for the modern guy who lives in an air-conditioned eighteenth-floor apartment, has had a vasectomy, and has fourteen girl friends he services like a bull does a herd.

We think we're so liberated and that we're free to do anything we want. But none of this liberation business is new. We didn't invent sex; we didn't invent sin. I mean, way back there in Sodom a guy shacked up with somebody's wife, and then over in Gomorrah they got drunk and were probably shooting morphine or whatever it was they did then. It's all been done before.

But then, somewhere down the line, the unwritten code of right and wrong came to the surface. Somebody said, "Wait a minute. I can't keep doing this because I don't sleep at night. Why don't I sleep at night? It's because I'm sleeping with somebody else's woman. I'm having a ball, but something's wrong."

And then one day a friend says to him, "You know what's wrong. Your conscience bothers you."

"What's my conscience?" asks the guy.

"Your conscience is whatever it is that's causing you not to sleep at night."

"What do you do about that?" asks the insomniac.

"I don't sleep with another man's woman."

So the guy goes out and for six months sleeps with his wife and no one else. Afterwards, he runs back to tell his friend, "You know, I have a little self-respect, and now I can sleep nights."

Deep down inside, we all know what's right and wrong. What's more, we all want to be part of the love that God has for us. For us to willingly separate ourselves from this fantastic deal he's given us seems almost inconceivable. And yet, like Adam and Eve, we do just that. We quickly succumb to the evil forces that are always there to tempt us.

But to have a chance at God's perfect love, you have to be on your guard all the time, because there's something out there that can get you and destroy you. Call it what you will, but I call it the devil. He's real, and he's waiting for us to slip up.

I see things in simple terms. To me, life is a lot like a garden. You can't go and leave a garden more than a week at most. If you do, things get into it: slugs, fungus, weeds. The earth gets too hard; it can't absorb moisture and the plants die.

The same is true of your faith, your children, your marriage, and everything of value in this life. You can't leave anything to chance or take anything for granted. Once you've embarked on a course, in order to be productive and fruitful it has to be constantly cared for. It's got to be such a part of your life that you have to give it constant attention.

One way I try to keep my garden tended is through prayer. Every single day I start out by thanking God, first of all for life and second of all for love. I'm thankful that I'm alive and thinking. And I'm thankful that life has love and the potential to exchange affection and sentiment and feeling and compassion with other people, because people are the most exciting things in the world. I end up my little prayer session by saying thanks for my family and friends.

Just starting the day thanking God for the simplest things gives me a lift. I pray anyplace—in a cab, on a plane, or in the barn with the cats. You don't have to throw yourself on the ground and go into great convulsions of praying. All you really need is one verse,

Psalms 118:24: "This is the day which the Lord has made; let us rejoice and be glad in it." (RSV)

The simple act of being thankful every day of your life makes you constantly aware that doing God's work is the most important thing in the world. It makes you aware that there's more to life than your own little problems and your own little desires, and that you really don't have to *worry* about anything because God's going to take care of it. Things may not always work out the way you expect them to, but in the end you'll come out ahead.

Letting God take charge doesn't mean that you give up on the everyday battles, or that there aren't moments and problems. It just means that there is an alternative offered to you, a way out if you are willing to look for it.

I've seen it in my own life. When I've been faced with crises or near-crises, there's always been a new opportunity offered to me by God. In some ways, my life has been like the cavalry in those Indian pictures where everybody was lost, there were only two wagons left and three shells were left in one gun. Then, at the very moment the Indians are whooping and hollering and poised to attack, miracle of miracles, the cavalry comes, "Ta, ta, ta, ta."

As a matter of fact, I regard my job at the *Today Show* as one of those miracles. Right before I was asked to come to New York, I had reached a point where some things in my life were beginning to build into crisis proportions. My weather job in Washington was one of them.

On the face of it, I looked like I had everything a man could ask for. I was making all the money I needed. Everything I owned was paid for. I had two great kids and a wife I considered my best friend. I had health and job recognition. After seventeen years as the local weatherman, I was a star in my own right, a "legend" in my own time, as they say. Who could have asked for anything more?

Yet, all that wasn't enough. My success had brought me to the point where I was bored out of my mind. I was nervous, and I was looking around for something else. But I really wasn't sure what I wanted to jazz up my life—another woman, another job, or whatever.

Then I was hit with lightning. Out of the blue, I was offered a chance to be the weatherman on the *Today Show*. I was sitting in my office in Washington one day when Bill Small, who was then the head of NBC News in New York, walked in. I had never met the guy before, but he came right over to me and introduced himself.

"I'm Bill Small from NBC News," he said. "Why haven't you ever been on the network?"

"Nobody ever asked me," I answered.

"How would you like to do the weather for the *Today Show*?" he said.

"I'd love it," I said.

That was it. Two months later I went to New York to do an on-air audition on the *Today Show* for two weeks during the Christmas of 1979. Not long after, I was hired as the weatherman.

I had needed something to change my life, and along came the biggest break in my career. I saw it as a gift of God.

CHAPTER 17

Willard Bites Into the Big Apple

One of my fondest moments in thirty-two years of broadcasting was on January 14, 1982. The occasion was the thirtieth anniversary of the *Today Show*. In the studio that day were nearly all the people who had been on the show at one time or another, including Dave Garroway, the first host.

At one point in the celebration, Garroway turned to Bryant Gumbel, who had just taken over as the new host the week before, and he said, "My friend, you are about to embark on a journey that will change the way you view the world."

After nearly two years on the *Today Show*, I knew exactly what he meant. The *Today Show* is more than a job. It's a way of life. Not only does the world take on a new meaning, but your personal life is affected in every way.

My personal journey began on Sunday, March 9, 1980, the day before I was to start as the regular weatherman on the *Today Show.*

Mary and I packed the station wagon like a bunch of Okies and drove along the Jersey Turnpike heading for New York City. We had rented a furnished apartment until we could get settled, but to feel more at home we were bringing along some of our own stuff.

I was excited, to put it mildly. Actually, I was thrilled to death by this new adventure, and I couldn't wait to become part of the life of the city.

To get a feel for what was happening on that Sunday, I turned on the car radio to all-news WCBS, a competing station. The first thing I heard was the sound of my own voice, doing a commercial for the Red Cross.

"Boy, am I hot stuff," I thought to myself. "Here I am, just a local weatherman from Washington, D.C., and I'm listening to myself on WCBS radio as I drive to New York City to do the *Today Show.*"

I still hadn't come down off my "high horse" by 4:30 Monday morning, when the limousine picked me up to take me to the NBC studios in the RCA building at Rockefeller Center.

It only took about fifteen minutes to get to the studio at that hour, and while New York slept, my mind was racing. But I wasn't thinking about my work that day. Instead, I was overcome by a flood of nostalgia, remembering back to another day, thirty-five years before, when I had made my first visit to New York City and the RCA building.

I had stopped in New York with my mother on the way to camp in New Hampshire. We had wanted to see the Empire State building, but the entire building had closed down because an Army B–25 had crashed into it a few weeks before. We took a tour of the RCA building instead.

That day was the first time I'd ever seen television. There was a demonstration of black-and-white TV in the RCA building, and part of the tour involved stopping to see this huge set with a little tiny screen. They were showing what television was going to be like as soon as the war was over. This was the new invention that was supposed to take America by storm.

I had been caught up in that storm, and now, like a dream, I was coming back to the very same place that had once overwhelmed me. I was part of it all. I had *made* it.

Or had I? Three months later I began to wonder. As I was standing by a bank of elevators in the RCA building with a fellow from NBC, we encountered some executives he knew in the company. He introduced me to a tall, shriveled-up man in his early seventies and an attractive younger woman in her fifties.

"How long have you been with NBC?" asked the woman.

"For thirty years," I said.

"And how long have you been in New York?" she asked.

"Three months," I said.

"Get out of here before they destroy you," she said.

I was stunned. Was this the success I had achieved? But as I thought back on those first three months in New York, I began to think that maybe she was right. Maybe a guy like me didn't fit into New York and would never belong.

I had already found myself getting caught up in the

incredible pace of network television, and I wasn't sure I liked it. It was a world of competition, big-time agents, deals, contracts, ego, and insecurity. All of that was unknown to me in Washington, which now seemed like a small town by comparison.

It was true, too, that during the first three months, I had gone through incredible highs and lows. The highs had zoomed me up into the ionosphere. In the first place, there was New York City itself, the Big Apple. The city was more beautiful, more open, and more receptive than I had ever imagined.

What amazed me most was that people were *honest*. Anyone who thinks that New Yorkers are out to take you to the cleaners at every turn ought to think again. If my experience is any example, even New York cab drivers can be angels in disguise.

Not long after I came to New York, I had to take a flight out of Kennedy Airport, which is about a forty-minute ride from my apartment. I knew there was construction on the highways going to Kennedy, so I left home an hour and a half early. Just four blocks away from my apartment, my cab got stuck in traffic for forty minutes, and I was sure I would never make the plane.

But as it turned out, once we made it past the tie-up, the cab driver barreled on out to Kennedy, and got me to the airport ten minutes before the plane left.

It was a $27 cab ride, and I gratefully handed the guy $40, telling him to keep the change. He wouldn't take it.

"That's too much," he said, and he handed me back $10.

I wasn't anybody special to him. I was just another

fare. But what made him special to me was that he was simply a decent human being.

That's what I found at every turn in New York City. I expected the city to be cold and aloof. But I've had the same response, the same feeling, on the streets of New York and in the halls of the RCA building that I had back home in Alexandria as a kid.

Call it warmth, call it love, you name it. All I know is that people in New York respond to it just like they did at the First Baptist Church in Alexandria. You give, and people give it back.

At first, though, the reaction I got from people at the RCA building was utter, absolute, total disbelief. What was even more horrifying to the New York sophisticates was my act on TV. I had toned down a lot from my Washington days, but I was still a cornball, a professional Southerner, and a wiseguy, and it was overwhelming.

But little by little, they responded. One morning I was walking along the hall when I came upon a young girl in her twenties. We looked at each other, and then immediately she turned her eyes away and tried to move ahead without acknowledging me.

She was a perfect stranger to me, but I wouldn't let her get away with that stony city stare.

"How are you this morning?" I said.

That was all she needed to warm up. She grabbed my arm and said, "My mother thinks you're great."

Now, that was a wonderful ego trip for me. But the real point of the story is that people are out there, ready to respond, even in a big city like New York. You meet thousands of strangers every day, but when your eyes meet, your heads go down, and nobody seems to give anybody a "howdy-do." They're afraid that it's corny to be nice or that the other person will take their friendliness the wrong way.

But I've found time after time that if you throw bread upon the water, it comes back, especially in New York. I start off with the premise that you *can* make a difference in other people's lives. You can be happy and cheerful and try to communicate that, or you can be as mean and as miserable as you want to be. You can walk into a party and have a chip on your shoulder and mess that party up and make it a disaster. Or you can walk into a group of people who are feeling kind of blah and without dominating the group, you can add a little something to make them feel brighter and happier.

If New York thrilled me with its unpredictable touches of humanity, my job on the *Today Show* was even more exciting. I mean, here I was, on national television, and I was working with what I considered the best team on the air. It was a real kick—almost as much fun as shelling peas.

When I started out, the team was headed up by Tom Brokaw, a good-looking guy who's smart, articulate, and aggressive as a journalist. Then there was co-anchor Jane Pauley, who along with being the best female news reader in television, is also the Midwest's darling, appealing to everybody as the girl next door. For color, there was Gene Shalit, who's intellectual, eccentric, fun, and has a tremendous sense of humor. Finally there was me—down-home, country, comfortable old Willard.

All the pieces fit. We all complemented each other beautifully, at least that's the way it appeared on television.

The first morning I walked into the studio, the place was like a tomb. Of course, it was early in the morning—*very* early—and everybody had a right to be groggy. But then I saw that even during the breaks in the show, when we had a few minutes to relax off camera while the film clips or commercials were on, you could still hear a pin drop. It was deadly silent.

I knew my act couldn't survive in that subdued atmosphere. I've always needed to make a little noise to get my adrenaline flowing before I go on camera, sort of the way a karate expert gives a shout before he hits somebody.

I've found that in the racket I'm in, you can't take your problems to work with you. TV is show business, and show business doesn't just begin with the camera. To get a good feeling on the air, you have to psych up the crew, psych up your colleagues, and psych up yourself. You have to laugh and giggle a little bit before you go on the air.

So, I started each morning by giving everybody a little bit of "Willard medicine," whether they wanted it or not. I'd begin by joking with the crew. As I walked by, I'd pat guys on the tail with a script or poke them in the ribs. They'd all laugh, and the atmosphere would loosen up.

During breaks in the show, I'd make wisecracks to Tom or Jane just to keep *myself* loose. While a commercial was running, I'd look over to Tom and say silly things like, "Your fly is open." He'd look down and start laughing. Or I'd say, "C'mon, you turkeys, let's go."

As a result, when the film clips were over and the camera came back to the four of us around the table, it looked to the folks at home like we had been telling jokes. All that had really happened, though, was that I had said something stupid.

I'm so loud and obnoxious that for some reason it calms people down. Jane Pauley told me that once. After a few weeks of my cheerleading, she said I helped her relax.

On the air, I tried to do the same for the viewers. I was as outrageous on the *Today Show* as I had been in Washington—doing things like dressing up like Cupid on Valentine's Day. I also continued my plugs for hometown events, such as the garden clubs, bazaars, and church barbecues that people had loved so much in Washington. I was adamant about keeping those in my act. To me, that was what I was all about, helping some of those six and a half million *Today Show* viewers feel like individuals; helping to bring the news down to a *human* level.

The way I see it, these plugs are little balls of love that I can send to the people at home. It's a way of communicating directly with the viewers, person to person. Once I got to the *Today Show* I added a new twist to these announcements: Along with naming organizations that have special events coming up, I name people who are celebrating landmark birthdays or anniversaries. If a couple has been married more than seventy-five years, I'll mention it on the air. There's something inspiring about marital staying power like that. Let's say they met when he was twenty and she was sixteen, and now they're celebrating their seventy-fifth anniversary. They've seen wars and depressions, and they've known wealth and death. Just by acknowledging this milestone in their lives, I can make a little personal statement about what's important in life, but without pontificating.

Gradually, people across the country responded to these messages just like they had in Washington, and I was deluged with requests to have this church fair mentioned or that annual petunia festival announced.

But despite the elation I felt by just being in New York, and by finding my niche on the show, there were times during those first few months when I hit rock bottom emotionally. I began to think that the only people who were truly happy in broadcasting were the kids making $75 a week working all night in a little 250-watt AM station. For them, the dream was still alive.

As for me, I was beginning to feel the pressures of competing in network television. It wasn't so much that I was in competition with anybody in particular. But the *Today Show* was in a ratings war with *Good Morning America*, and I felt it at every turn.

At a local station like WRC in Washington, the ratings come out a couple of times a year. Everything is geared toward those ratings periods and immediately afterwards there's either elation or depression, depending on the results. A few people may get fired and some changes may be made, but after a few weeks, things settle back to normal.

At the network, everything's accelerated. Ratings come out every week for shows like the *Today Show*, so you can tell from week to week whether you're bombing out or making it. The result is that every week your emotions can go up and down like a yo-yo.

As if these outside pressures weren't bad enough, there were also corporate pressures within NBC that affected the way the *Today Show* operated. There are two factions within the NBC News Division that are constantly warring over the direction of the show. One group thinks the show should be more news-oriented, while the other leans more toward entertainment.

All of this competition creates a crisis atmosphere, which puts the stars of the show under constant pressure to perform. No matter how much you believe in yourself, you can quickly become insecure and defensive, and you begin to think only of one thing—self-preservation.

Gradually, I saw myself succumbing to these pressures, and I didn't like the person I was becoming.

My first hint that I might be on thin ice on the show came a few weeks after I started, when I inadvertently discovered that some of my mail was being kept from me.

When I first came on the show, I was deluged with mail. Almost all the letters were positive, and so I thought everything was terrific. The problem was, a good portion of the mail was negative, but those letters had been hidden from me by some well-meaning staff people. They didn't tell me about them because they thought it would hurt my feelings. But when I discovered the cover-up, I was surprised and angry.

"How can you possibly get an honest appraisal of what's happening if you don't see what the complaints are?" I said.

To me, the negative mail wasn't something to be ashamed of. It was an opportunity to communicate with people. The most significant thing about the mail, as far as I was concerned, was the volume. I was getting 1,000 letters a week, more than anyone else on the show. It didn't bother me one bit that about a third of those were negative, because as I said, what counts in television isn't so much that people like you, it's that they *remember* you.

Most of the negative mail was from people who attacked my size. They couldn't believe that NBC had let a fat person like me on the air. Combine that with the gap between my teeth and the fact that I lumber a little when I walk, and I was a ready-made target for criticism.

I knew that I had a problem on my hands, and the problem seemed to be me.

As if the bad news from the viewers wasn't enough, there were also pressures on the show which were putting me on edge. In the first place, my time on the air always seemed to be getting cut. I'd be in the middle of my weather report, and from behind the camera I'd constantly get a speed-up signal, urging me to get my part over with so they could move on to the rest of the show. For example, instead of getting two-and-a-half minutes of air time at a shot, I'd be told to cut back to one-minute-thirty-seconds.

Now, the loss of a minute of air time may not seem like the end of the world. But I saw it as a direct threat to my career. The more time I had on the air, the better I was able to create an easy-going image. That friendly informality was my strength. If they took that away from me, it would be like cutting Samson's hair.

I'd been in the business long enough to know that nine times out of ten they didn't really have a time problem. They just wanted to keep the show moving in the beginning, and take up the slack at the end if they had to.

But I also knew I had to do something fast to preserve my integrity on the air. I waited until the show was over one day and grabbed one of the executives by the arm.

"Have you seen what's happening to me?" I asked. When he said he didn't know what I was talking about, I unleashed my fury.

"You're not going to mess up my career by cutting my time," I told him. Then I gave him an ultimatum.

"If you ever do that to me again," I said, "I'm going to walk out the door and I'll never come back. I can't do what I was brought up here to do without some leeway."

Along with my conflicts on the show, there were new problems I had to deal with in my personal life, as I tried to adjust to the crazy hours I had to keep. To be ready for the show at 7:00 A.M., I had to wake up at 4:00 A.M. Often, I'd work straight through until two or three in the afternoon. Other times, we kept going until nine or ten at night.

It was even worse when we did the show from another time zone. In California, for example, I got up at 1 A.M. to go on the air at four, which was 7 A.M. New York time.

During those first few months on the show, I was groping for some kind of schedule that would give me the semblance of a normal life. But nothing seemed to work, and my topsy-turvy existence was affecting everybody around me. Some nights, Mary and I would plan a nice quiet evening at home together, and at 8:30 P.M. I'd find myself falling asleep in the middle of a conversation.

On weekends, I'd race home to my farm in Virginia, where my idea of a big time was to go upstairs and go to bed. Of course, then I'd wake up at 4:00 A.M., and I'd be so restless I'd go down to the kitchen and putter around. The dogs would hear me and start barking, and before long, everyone in the house was awake and mad at me.

Our social life suffered, too. When I'd decline a dinner invitation, saying that if I came, I'd have to leave early to get to sleep, the hostess would invariably say, "Oh, come and stay for as long as you can—we'll understand."

But they never did. If you go, they don't understand why you poop out before dinner is served, and if you don't go at all they think you're snubbing them. So, you lose all the way around. And what you lose most is sleep.

Now, this may seem like a minor problem, but believe me, it was making my life miserable. Finally, I solved the problem by taking an afternoon nap, which meant I could stay up until 11:00 P.M. But it took me months to figure that out.

My problems adjusting to the show were compounded by new headaches I had to deal with now that I was at the "top" of the profession. As the weeks went on, it became more and more apparent that I needed an agent to help me deal with the muckety-mucks at NBC.

Now, I don't want to deprive anyone of a living. But it simply offended my sense of honor to have to pay some guy $40,000-a-year to be my representative and say to my bosses the very same things I could say myself. Where I come from, all I needed was a handshake and a simple contract to keep my job and be secure.

But at NBC headquarters in New York it was a new ball game, and agents were the name of the game.

I look at agents the way some people look at bankers.

My attitude is summed up in an old joke about a banker with a glass eye: When you look at a banker who's wearing a glass eye, how can you tell which one is the glass eye and which is the real eye? You look at the one with the slightest touch of human kindness—and that's the glass eye.

Yes, some agents *are* a lot like bankers.

Then, of course, there's comedian Fred Allen's comment that "All the sincerity of broadcasting would fit in the navel of a gnat. After that, there'd still be room left over for your agent's heart."

Those jokes sounded funny once. But now that I needed an agent, they seemed all too true.

I began to feel like I was on an emotional roller coaster, not knowing from one day to the next whether I had made the smartest move of my career or the dumbest mistake of my life by coming to the *Today Show*. One day I'd finish the show and everything would be going well, the next day everything seemed to fall apart. On days like that, I'd rush out of the studio and just walk the streets, wondering whether to tough it out in New York, or to pack it all in and go home to my farm in Virginia.

From week to week it was the same. On Mondays I'd be able to see things in some sort of perspective, but by Wednesday things would have gone completely haywire. I'd read a negative review about me in some magazine, or I'd overhear a crack about me in the halls, and I'd fold up and dissolve. A couple of days later, I'd get a nice review somewhere, and I'd come back up again.

Things got to such a state that I started to take a tranquilizer before I went on the air every morning. I happened to mention this to Jane one day and she couldn't believe that I was nervous. She seemed even more astounded that I had mentioned it. But I wasn't ashamed. I was just trying to figure the whole thing out.

At the start of every show, I'd be sitting watching the teleprompter, and as it rolled closer to my weather report, I'd start to get short of breath. Then I'd think about how terrible it would be if I fainted on the air, and I'd feel even worse.

So to keep myself calm, I held a tranquilizer in my hand until thirty seconds before I went on the air. Then I'd pop it in my mouth. After that, I was fine for the rest of the show.

The irony is that I'm not a pill-taking type. I almost never take even aspirin. Even more ironic is the fact that I can be out of town, before a live crowd of 2,000 people, and I don't need a thing. But there's something about the pressure in the studio in New York that just got to me, like it never had before.

I was at the top level of a field that was an incredibly high-pressure business. There were tremendous risks involved, and tremendous stakes in the game. I wasn't sure whether I was winning, but I knew I was paying the price.

My one refuge from it all was the farm in Virginia, where I went every Friday after the show. At home, I settled back into the uncomplicated life I loved more than anything else in this world. Gradually I began to realize that I had nothing to lose in New York, because the two things that really meant anything to me were my family and my farm. I could give up everything else, even the *Today Show*, and still be content.

But as things turned out, I didn't have to give up anything. I got it *all*. The first tip-off that things were beginning to go my way was a comment a guy made to me on an NBC elevator. I don't even know who he was. He wasn't a big executive in a pinstripe suit. He was a technician.

At any rate, the two of us were alone in the elevator, and as we were going down he looked at me and confessed, "You know, I was on the elevator with you the first day they hired you. At the time, I said to myself, " 'What the heck have they done? Have they lost their minds?' "

With that, he put on a big grin and said, "You know, I really like you."

I felt like hugging the guy. Here was a convert, a guy who understood that I wasn't trying to put across some phony act but was just trying to be a human being on the screen. That message had finally come through to one person, at least. It was a beginning.

Oddly enough, from then on, it seemed that hardly a day went by without somebody coming up to me with a nice comment. Not only that, my mail suddenly started turning around. Out of the hundreds of letters I was getting every week, only about ten or so were bad. About half of the people who had written me hate mail in the beginning wrote back to say, "You're getting better. Keep it up."

Before long, the media got on the bandwagon. First there was a cover story on the show in *Time* magazine that was very complimentary to me, and then I had a string of positive articles in the in-flight magazines of the major airlines. It was a tremendous ego boost. But the icing on the cake was an article on television weathermen in the *Los Angeles Times*, which referred to me as "the big friendly man who's become a national folk hero."

They were talking about *me*. I couldn't believe it.

Little by little, all this heady stuff started to sink in. But it wasn't until the Republican National Convention in Detroit that it finally dawned on me that I was a national celebrity of sorts.

We were doing the *Today Show* live from Detroit's Renaissance Center every morning, and it was the first time I had been out of town with the show. My job was to do a variety of weather spots from various places in Detroit and around the convention site. Wherever I went, I noticed that people on the streets kept hollering out to me, "Hi Willard," or "We love you, Willard."

I figured that since this was the Republican National Convention, the people who were calling out must have been some of my old fans from Washington. I was still a little puzzled by exactly what was happening when I happened to walk into a hotel bar one night and people broke into cheers. I spotted a group of Washington people over in a corner, and again I figured the cheers had come from the old Washington crowd. Although I was pleased, I shrugged it off.

But when a crowd showed up to watch the show one morning waving placards, I finally got the message. The signs read: "Jane is a 10, Tom is a 10, Willard is an 11."

These people weren't from Washington. They weren't politicians. They were just plain folks, and best of all, they were my fans. I was overwhelmed.

The acclaim of the crowd in Detroit was one thing. But I really knew I'd made it when Ann Landers called to ask me for advice! She wanted to know my definition of "Midwest." A lot of people from Missouri and Kansas were unhappy, she said, because TV weather people kept referring to the Midwest as Ohio and Indiana.

I told her that I called Ohio and Indiana the "Ohio

Valley" or the "Middle Mississippi Valley," and that when I talked about the Midwest I meant the heartland—Missouri, Iowa, Nebraska, and Kansas. She not only listened, she printed it.

As if Ann Landers weren't enough, there was Johnny Carson, who referred to me in his opening monologue one night as the "Wide, Wide World of Willard." Any doubts I had about whether I could make it in New York on the *Today Show* were quickly erased from my mind.

But when I was asked to cover the Macy's Thanksgiving Day Parade for the *Today Show*, I was convinced I was about to enter heaven.

Some people may not think that the Macy's parade is the pinnacle of success, but to me, covering that parade was probably the highlight of my professional career. It was the kind of thing I had looked forward to ever since I was a kid, working as a page at WRC. Just to be there, right on Broadway, broadcasting live from the heart of Manhattan, made me feel so proud. I was interviewing celebrities and special acts who were going to be marching later that morning, and I was having a ball.

This was what America was all about: high school bands, Mickey Mouse, the Rockettes, and Superman. There was something heroic about the whole thing. As I worked the crowd that day, I remembered how Herman and Thelma had told me about the parade when I was a kid. And I thought how proud they would have been to see me there at that moment. Here I was, right smack in the middle of it. I was helping to make it happen. It was a fantasy come true.

To me, covering the parade represented my own personal miracle on Thirty-fourth Street. I could have left

New York a winner that day and never come back. I could have walked away, totally happy that I had accomplished everything I ever wanted out of life.

There was only one challenge left for me to take on— myself.

CHAPTER 18

A New Today;
A New Willard

When diet guru Nathan Pritikin walked on the *Today Show* one April morning in 1981, he took one look at me, sized me up like a piece of meat, and probably thought to himself, "If I could get hold of this guy, I'd get a free advertisement forever."

I took one look at him and immediately came under his spell. What drew me to him were his eyes. They were incredibly penetrating, and almost hypnotic in their power.

Pritikin is a very persuasive man, and what he had to say about health and diet that day made a lot of sense. I had been thinking about trying to lose weight for a couple of years, but up until then I hadn't really gotten

214

serious about it. Part of me had decided that I was a lost cause, and also I figured that since I had gotten this far in television without being a matinee idol, I might as well stay fat and happy.

There was another part of me, though, that wasn't completely happy with what I saw in the mirror every morning. I'd look at myself and say, "What a fool. You're a nice man. You've got nice skin. You've got a wonderful job on national television. People like you. Why don't you try to look a little nicer? Why do you go out of your way to be a fat slob?"

I couldn't really answer those questions. What I did know was that I was forty-seven years old and I wasn't getting any younger. What's more, my feet and knees had started to hurt, and I thought maybe the 285 pounds I carried around was the reason. That got me thinking about the people I'd known who had had heart attacks and strokes and I saw myself as a candidate for physical disaster.

When I looked at myself closely, I realized I wasn't just letting nature take its course, I was helping it along. I was allowing myself to go to pot, not only by eating too much, but by continuing to drink. I didn't drink much during the day, but when evening rolled around, I'd sit back and enjoy my "cocktail hour" which often stretched on longer than I'd like to say.

But I was starting to get sick of booze. I had seen what had happened to Herman with his drinking, and after a while something inside me clicked. I also began to think about my daughters, who were now legally old enough to drink, and I figured that maybe I owed it to them to set a better example. They had been around my cocktail hour all of their lives, and you know how it is

215

with kids—"monkey see, monkey do." I figured that if I quit, perhaps when they got to be my age, they'd remember what I had done and do the same.

So, when that April morning rolled around, I was mentally ready to make a bold change in my life. All I needed was a catalyst, and the sixty-five-year-old Pritikin was *it*.

On the show, Pritikin explained how at the age of forty he had been a cardiac cripple. He had been a lean, active guy, and yet he had lost all his energy and nearly his life because his heart was in such bad shape. The blood vessels leading to his heart were so clogged with cholesterol that his heart could barely function.

His doctor told him the problem was hereditary and that the only solution was to limit his activities. He had to nap every afternoon, walk no more than four blocks a day, and take it easy for the rest of his life.

Pritikin was no dummy, and he knew it was only a matter of time before he would be six feet under. But he wasn't ready to give up the ghost that easily. At the time, he was an independent inventor and researcher, and one of his pet interests was nutrition. So, he decided to take a closer look at his diet for an answer to his medical problems.

What he found was that his diet was a disaster. He was eating red meat, oils, and dairy foods that were literally clogging his system with cholesterol. He figured right then and there that the only thing hereditary about the heart disease that had crippled his family for years was that his mother and grandmothers had taught their kids how to eat.

So, Pritikin gave up his all-American eating habits and came up with a radical low-cholesterol diet that could, and did, extend his life. It took him fifteen years to rid his body of heart disease, but there he was, on the *Today Show*, a living testimony to the success of his methods.

The more Pritikin talked, the more ready I was to try to get in shape. If he could come back from death's door, maybe it wouldn't be so hard for me, since I wasn't *that* bad off, *yet*. After the show, he took my name and address, and a month later he showed up at my farm in Virginia, where he spent a Sunday afternoon convincing me to get started on a diet and getting Mary to help me stick to it.

There was one thing holding me back. "If I lose weight," I said, "I'm going to spoil my image."

"If you don't start spoiling your image, you're not going to be here to worry about it," he retorted. "Take it from me, people will like you a lot better handsome than fat."

His diet, he said, was simple. He told me that his big emphasis was on eating carbohydrates, such as whole grains, fruits, vegetables, beans, and potatoes. The idea was to stuff yourself all day with foods that are low in calories and high in bulk so you won't get hungry. Under his system, he said, I could eat pasta, cereal, and all the bread I wanted. Since I've always been a big bread eater, that sounded good to me.

Protein, particularly red meat, was a big no-no, said Pritikin, and I had to limit myself to no more than a pound and a half a week of lean meat, fish, and fowl. Fats and oils were an even bigger no-no. Pritikin is such a fanatic that he doesn't even eat peanuts because they have too much oil in them. I didn't have to go that far, he said, but I did have to give up the dairy foods I loved most: rich cheeses, thick coats of butter, and farm-fresh eggs. But I kept listening.

What really sold me on Pritikin's plan, though, was that he left me a way out. After spending an afternoon with me, he figured I'd never stick to his diet if I didn't have some chance to cheat. After all, who wants to go through Christmas without fruitcake or Little Mary's and Sally's cookies?

So before he left, he leaned over and with his mouth askew in a wry little smile, he said, "If you make it 75 to 80 percent of the way through this diet, you're going to be all right."

That was all it took to convert me. But not only was I won over to Pritikin's principles, I also added a big one of my own. I gave up cocktail hour. Pritikin's smart enough to know that he wouldn't get many converts if he outlawed liquor from his diet. So he says you can have a drink, although he admits the calories are wasted. What he emphasizes instead is exercise and proper nutrition.

Between no booze and Pritikin's diet, within a matter of months I had lost forty pounds. I went from a size 52 suit to a size 46, my knees and feet stopped hurting, and I felt like I was Clark Gable.

I've stuck to the diet ever since, with one or two little modifications of my own. Some of his suggestions, like a salad dressing made with bean curd, I really couldn't stomach. The stuff tasted awful, like a loose oyster, except a loose oyster has a little more flavor. Once a week I cheat and have an egg and some red meat, but the rest of the time I follow his advice to the letter.

What's more, I even joined a health club. Can you imagine me, Willard Scott, in a health club? Pritikin had told me to walk an hour a day, but I did him one better. Now I get regular exercise, and I've never slept better in my life. My mind even works faster. Soon after I went on my new regime, I discovered that I felt a lot more calm and that my short-term memory had actually improved. For example, I used to be terrible at remembering phone numbers. Now I can remember them with no trouble at all.

I'm not getting older, I'm getting better!

I've been in New York only a couple of years, and I feel like I've already come out ahead. This is the great city that's supposed to corrupt, but I've gotten so corrupt that now I belong to a health club and get regular exercise. I came to "sin city," and I lose weight and stop drinking.

The "new Willard" not only made me feel good about myself, it made other people feel good about me too. To a lot of people, I'm like the Prodigal Son, who once was a naughty boy but who now has confessed his sins and is welcomed back with open arms by his family. That's how the viewers have responded to me since I lost all that weight.

Typical is a letter I got from a doctor in Chicago. He told me bluntly that when I first came on the show, he didn't like me because I was loud and disruptive. But the real reason he didn't like me was that I was fat.

"The fact that you were obese completely turned me off," he wrote.

Then the doctor confessed that after I lost forty pounds, he did an about-face. "Now," he wrote, "I'm your ardent fan and you're the only reason I watch the show anymore. You're an inspiration to America."

I never realized the tremendous impact that my losing weight could have on others. But the effect has been dramatic. I find that wherever I am, fat people come up to me and say, "How did you do it? Tell me, tell me, because I want to do it too."

All of this positive feedback has given a tremendous boost to my career. On the *Today Show,* I have a sense of confidence that I've never had before. Maybe part of that confidence comes from the fact that I'm now entrenched as one of the "old-timers" on the show. I've seen one anchorman leave, and a new anchor team come in, ushering in a dramatic new direction to the program.

With Bryant Gumbel, the program has taken on a new relaxed atmosphere, more like what it was when it first started out in the fifties. Then it was primarily a "show," an entertaining eye-opener that was relaxed and comfortable to watch.

The new *Today* still has news, of course, with Chris Wallace, who's young and aggressive. But the whole mood of the show has shifted to a fun, easygoing style that fits me to a tee.

Between the new *Today* and the new Willard, I feel so positive about life that I'm ready to take on the world. It may be coincidence, but not long after I got "thin" some of the bigwigs at NBC started talking to me about doing my own morning talk show in addition to doing the *Today Show.*

One of the most positive things that has happened to me is that I've had a chance to travel all over the country with the show. Since I started with the *Today Show,* I've been in more than thirty cities, and everywhere I go I feel close to the people I meet.

But in all my travels, the place where I felt most at home was a little town called Paducah, Kentucky. I was there in the fall of 1981 to do a telethon. Every year, the local NBC affiliate, WPSD-TV, puts on an incredible telethon to raise money for crippled children, and they invited me down to spend six or seven hours on the air.

Afterwards, I went to a big tent to join some of the people who had come by to contribute.

The people in Paducah were 100 percent rural rolks, and as I sat there in that tent chatting with them, I felt like I was back with my own family. Those people were so much like my aunts and uncles. Everything about them reminded me of the North Carolina crowd in my mother's family. There was just something in the way they looked and the way they talked.

To make me really feel at home during my visit, they actually made me an honorary Duke of Paducah, and, of course, they also made me an honorary Kentucky Colonel.

But that's the way it's been all over the country. I've been received so warmly that I've become almost an adopted son in every city I've visited.

To me, the entire country is now like one big neighborhood. I can go down a street in Denver, Colorado, and people will holler at me just like they do in my hometown of Alexandria. And I must confess that I love it.

Whenever I get too full of myself, though, I think about the little cemetery plot Mary and I own over in the Episcopal Parish graveyard in Leeds, Virginia. There's a certain sanity in cemeteries.

Our plot is a beautiful, grassy spot, surrounded by trees. It's just a small piece of real estate, but while it's appreciating, I'm depreciating!

I think about that, and I come back down to earth. That plot is a reminder that none of the things I've achieved will last forever. Like everyone else in the world, I'm living on borrowed time. When that time runs out, it really won't matter whether I'm fat or thin, famous or anonymous, rich or poor.

The only thing that will matter will be how I lived

the life I was given: How much joy I got out of it, how much love I put into it, and whether I made peace with God.

When you get right down to it, the most important events in your life are the day you're born and the day you die. That's why, every now and then, Mary and I pay a visit to Leeds Parish. We sit in our little plots and have a picnic, all by ourselves, because that's where we're going to be for the rest of eternity.

What we love most is just sitting there quietly, watching the sunset.

The way I have it figured, we're going to be there for a long time, so we might as well *enjoy* it.